PROTECTION WITH POWER

PROTECTION
– WITH –
POWER

What Financial
Professionals May Not
Want You to Know

DOUGLAS A. CLANCY, JR.

NEW YORK

LONDON • NASHVILLE • MELBOURNE • VANCOUVER

PROTECTION WITH POWER
What Financial Professionals May Not Want You to Know

© 2023 DOUGLAS A. CLANCY, JR.

Published in New York, New York, by Morgan James Publishing. Morgan James is a trademark of Morgan James, LLC. www.MorganJamesPublishing.com

Proudly distributed by Publishers Group West®

Morgan James BOGO™

A **FREE** ebook edition is available for you or a friend with the purchase of this print book.

CLEARLY SIGN YOUR NAME ABOVE

Instructions to claim your free ebook edition:
1. Visit MorganJamesBOGO.com
2. Sign your name CLEARLY in the space above
3. Complete the form and submit a photo of this entire page
4. You or your friend can download the ebook to your preferred device

ISBN 9781683505693 paperback
ISBN 9781683505709 eBook
Library of Congress Control Number:
2017907093

Cover Design by:
Rachel Lopez
www.r2cdesign.com

Interior Design by:
Bonnie Bushman
The Whole Caboodle Graphic Design

Morgan James is a proud partner of Habitat for Humanity Peninsula and Greater Williamsburg. Partners in building since 2006.

Get involved today! Visit: www.morgan-james-publishing.com/giving-back

DISCLAIMER

All written content is for information purposes only. It is not intended to provide any tax or legal advice or provide the basis for any financial decisions. Opinions expressed herein are solely opinions of the author Douglas A. Clancy, Jr.

All information and ideas should be discussed in detail with your individual advisor or a qualified professional before making any financial decisions. We are not affiliated with or endorsed by any government agency.

Douglas A. Clancy, Jr. is president of Retirement Planning Services, Inc. dba Cornerstone Wealth & Tax Advisory Group, a registered investment advisor in the state of California.

Douglas A. Clancy, Jr. is president of CSWTA Insurance Solutions, California Insurance Agency # 0H27254. Douglas A. Clancy, Jr., California Insurance License # 0G20617.

Retirement Planning Services, Inc. dba Cornerstone Wealth & Tax Advisory Group in CA and CSWTA Insurance Solutions are affiliated companies.

The content in this book is the sole opinion of Douglas A. Clancy, Jr.

Whenever you invest, you are at risk of loss of principal, as the market does fluctuate. Past performance is not indicative of future results. Purchases are subject to suitability. This requires a review of an investor's objective, risk tolerance, and time horizons. Investing always involves risk and possible loss of capital.

The information contained herein is not an offer to sell or a solicitation of an offer to buy the securities, products, or services mentioned, and no offers or sales will be made in jurisdictions in which the offer or sale of these securities, products, or services is not qualified or otherwise exempt from regulation.

DEDICATION

This book is dedicated to the two most important women in my life—my mom, Doris E. Clancy, and my loving wife, Lisa M. Clancy.

My mom was taken from us much too early, but she touched many lives in her short time on earth. Truly an amazing person. To this day she is the most positive, upbeat person that I have ever known. I never heard her say a bad word about anyone.

She gave me the courage to be me. She taught me to be direct, and to help those in need. Mom, I miss you every day, every hour, and every minute.

My wife, Lisa, and I have been together for more than twenty years. She is my rock, my best friend, my business partner, and the love of my life. Lisa has been such a positive force in running our business—her background as a former CPA and corporate controller has been extremely valuable in many ways.

On a personal note, thank you, Lisa. Your love and compassion drive me to work hard for our clients and our family every day.

I am forever in the debt of these two-amazing people.

Love,

Doug

TABLE OF CONTENTS

ACKNOWLEDGMENTS

Thank you, Lisa M. Clancy, my lovely wife. Thank you for always having confidence in me. You are my rock, the love of my life, and my best friend.

Thank you to my son, Eric Clancy. I love you, son. Continue being you. Always be open to learning. Stay humble. Continue to do the *next* right thing. People helping people!

Thank you,

Douglas A. Clancy, Jr.

AUTHOR'S NOTE

I have met with thousands of people over my twenty-plus years in the finance business. From talking to so many wonderful people, I've learned that many people have misconceptions or questions about their investments.

I decided to write this book to point out some of those misconceptions so that you can be aware of them, and to make it easier for you to understand investing.

—Doug

ABOUT

PROTECTION WITH POWER

As you get closer to retirement, you may be starting to think about what you're going to spend your nest egg on. You may have plans for lifelong dreams and adventures, or something that you want to do for your children or loved ones.

You've invested more than just money into your retirement accounts—you've invested many years of your time, and made countless sacrifices over those years, all to reap the fruits of your labor one day and leave a legacy that you can be proud of.

Perhaps you've made shrewd investments in the market and seen your retirement accounts grow. Many people weren't so lucky and felt the pain of losing much of their savings when the market turned down in 2008, forcing them to go back to work or to delay retirement. Due to factors completely out of their control, many never got to reap the benefits of their golden years or leave the fruits of their labor to their beneficiaries.

Doug Clancy has spent the last twenty-plus years of his life as a financial and insurance advisor helping people navigate the tumultuous seas of investing for retirement. In *Protection with Power*, Doug has distilled his knowledge about investing into a message clear enough for anyone to understand. Read on and you will get to know Doug as well.

Doug is here to teach you that it **is** possible to keep some of your money safe *and* to participate in the upside of the market, **without paying outrageous fees**. However, to accomplish this, you need the right investment strategy and the right financial professionals working in your best interest.

Do you want to learn how to keep some part of your money safe? *Protection with Power* will help teach you.

INTRODUCTION

Understanding money isn't as hard as many may think it is or even as hard as some may want you to think.

I pride myself on explaining investing for retirement to people in a way that they can understand—including the things many leave out. Many financial professionals skip over the downsides of investments they're selling, asking you to "trust" them. When I first got into the business, I was handed training materials. I had no idea how difficult the new terms for my new career would be to understand. I also recognized that helping potential clients understand their choices and options would be difficult as the material was laid out. I kept racking my brain thinking of ways to clearly get my message across so that potential clients could make an informed decision for what they felt was best for them. My feeling was, so what if I understand it? I've been thrown several books and training manuals, but no one cared much for explaining these choices and options to potential clients. At this time, presentation software had come on the scene. I enjoy learning, so I dived into learning how to make presentations. I took a flight cross-country from Manchester, New Hampshire, to San Diego, California, with a new laptop in hand and the software on my computer.

I started jotting down on paper my thoughts for designing a presentation that did two things: (1) covered the benefits of the plan I was offering, and (2) included any limitations.

You will not believe this, but the presentation worked so well that the company I worked for asked me if they could mass produce it for the entire office.

I am always happy to be a team player and help others, so I easily said yes. In return, the next day, my old boss came into my office and took me to lunch, but before heading back to the office we stopped at the golf store. As a thank you he told me to pick out any set of golf clubs I wanted. I chose King Cobra's.

I was happy and more importantly my new clients were happy. They had a plan that worked for them, a plan they understood and participated in.

It's important for an advisor to know the plans they are offering. In my opinion, it's just as important for the client to understand their plan and not just trust the advisor. This is the reason I feel I have had great success in this business. An ability to not only understand the plans I offer, but also learn and understand plans my competitors offer.

I'm not a guy who puts myself on a pedestal. I talk *to* you—not *over* you. I don't wear ties. I don't wear jackets. You'll usually find me in a pair of slacks and a .polo shirt and, yes, sometimes jeans. I'm just a regular guy who has put time and effort into learning my craft. I believe in educating as opposed to selling.

Because the industry is built to control information, it's important to find someone who can explain to you what your money is doing so that **you** can understand it—not just so that they say *they* can.

If a financial professional can't explain to you why something works in a way that you can understand, it doesn't mean that he or she is smarter than you—it's a red flag. If someone makes it seem complicated, he's being less smart. If one can make investing seem simple, it's probably because he understands it better.

Who do you want to manage your money—someone who can relate to you? Or someone who claims to be an "expert" but can't explain the reasons behind what he recommends for you?

I'm never the smartest person in the room. I simply love helping people invest for retirement. I work hard to do it as well as I can, just as a doctor, a nurse, a construction worker, a mechanic, or any other kind of specialist puts time and dedication into honing their craft. I can't do those things. But I can educate you on keeping your money secure. That's what I love to do.

Our money is important to all of us, whether we have $1,000 or $100 million. It affects our lifestyle, our health, and our happiness. There is even a strong correlation between stock market declines and hospital admissions for anxiety.[1]

Our money is serious business, and managing it can be stressful.

We work hard to earn our money—studying a profession, mastering our craft, and going into work every day to deliver value to our clients—and to provide for ourselves and our families.

Yet when it comes to managing that money, it's easy to turn a blind eye. After all, it's scary!

"We know better than you," its practitioners say. "We'll take care of it."

No wonder it's hard to get information on what's happening with your money!

While I'm a part of the same industry, I don't subscribe to that philosophy. My philosophy in finance—as in life—is much simpler and clearer. I believe that good financial advice can be easy to understand if I do my job well.

My job, as I see it, is to help you understand the ins and outs of what your money is doing when you invest, including the all-important "facts." My philosophy doesn't come from an ivory tower of financial knowledge. It comes from mentors who taught me the meaning of honesty and clarity.

1   Alan Farnham, "When Stocks Drop, Heart Attacks Rise," *ABC News*, January 7, 2014, http://abcnews.go.com/Business/stocks-decline-heart-attacks-increase/story?id=21434968.

I have been fortunate to rely on many mentors in my life: teachers, coaches, and influential people who helped shape my morals, ethics, and ideals. One mentor stands out from all the others; he taught me about money, sure, but he also taught me so much about life.

That mentor is my father.

Douglas A. Clancy, Sr. was firm but fair; an old-school parent who loved my sisters and me without question. My father worked hard, but he always gave me love and attention. For much of my childhood, he had more than one job, but that never stopped him from attending my hockey games or school events. He gave me all I could ever ask for and more.

Still, he wasn't afraid to administer a swift smack on the rear end when I caused trouble. Truth be told, I wasn't afraid of the smack. Scolding cut deeper. A harsh word meant that I'd disappointed one of the people I loved most in the world.

All the lessons he taught me over the years earned my love and respect, but one lesson about the clear divide between right and wrong sticks out in my mind to this day.

Before online banking and mobile apps, you had to go to the bank in person to cash your paycheck. My father usually went on Fridays, cashing his check and then heading straight to the grocery store to feed the hungry mouths waiting at home.

One afternoon I accompanied my father. We waited our turn in a long line. After what felt like an eternity, we reached the teller. My father cashed his check and got his money, and we were on our way out the door.

I was excited to be out of there and on to the grocery store. I was already coming up with ways to convince him to get me an ice cream. Then my father turned around and told me we had to get back in line.

"Why?" I asked. I tried to hide that I was upset, but it was a struggle. I was so ready to be out of there!

"The bank made a mistake."

I wasn't thrilled. We were in New Hampshire, and it was one of the three nice days that we were allotted each year. I'd rather have been eating ice cream and playing ball. But I bit my tongue, and we got back in line.

When we reached the teller again, my father put two twenty-dollar bills down on the counter. "You just cashed my check," he reminded the teller. "But you gave me the wrong amount of money."

The teller looked as if he was on the wrong end of a long day. His weary face conveyed that he just wanted to get his shift over with and get home.

Still, as politely as the teller could muster, he said, "Sir, there's nothing I can do for you. We already cashed your check."

My father insisted. "It's the wrong amount."

The teller's frustration started to seep out. "Sir, I explained to you already: We already cashed it. The transaction is closed out."

I watched my father calmly push the money toward the teller, who must have been too tired to catch his drift.

My father patiently explained, "There were a couple of extra twenties stuck together. I don't want you to lose your job."

The teller's stunned expression was burned into my memory in that moment. The collision of shock and gratitude etched in his features will stick with me forever.

We lived about twenty minutes from the grocery store, and as we drove back home, my father explained to me why it was so important that he returned, waited in line, and made things right.

"If I had walked out of there with that extra money, son, it would have been stealing—even if it was the bank's mistake," He said. "If you steal one dollar, or you steal a million dollars, you're still a thief."

This moment was so representative of the example that my father—both of my parents, really—set for me throughout my formative years. They taught me to always be truthful and to always own up to my mistakes.

They gave me the confidence to know that if I did the right thing, then everything would always be OK—even if admitting to an infraction got me grounded for a weekend.

I've carried the philosophy of being honest and direct throughout my career as a financial advisor. I won't compromise my morals or ethics for any company or any person.

I always make sure to treat everyone with respect and courtesy, and we look out for our clients' needs primarily. In an ideal world, everyone would operate that way—but unfortunately, the world we live in is far from ideal.

Think of the movie *The Wolf of Wall Street*, which is based on a true story.[2] Matthew McConaughey plays a successful stockbroker named Mark Hanna, who is teaching a young Jordan Belfort (played by Leonardo DiCaprio) about Wall Street.

Hanna tells Belfort that the goal of a stockbroker is to "move the money from your client's pocket to your pocket."

The inexperienced Belfort asks Hanna if it is good for the clients to make money. Hanna responds simply and tellingly:

"No."

To counter Belfort's shock, Hanna goes on to explain that *selling* is the most important part of being a stockbroker—not helping the clients make money.

The recent market crashes of 2000 and 2008, threats of war or unrest, the housing crisis: These are all situations where people bought things without properly weighing the facts.

There are no magic investments. Everything has pros and cons—another side, consequence, or risk to consider. If you've been told only what you want to hear, only the upsides, then it's very likely that you're overlooking the downsides.

---

2   *Wolf of Wall Street*, directed by Martin Scorsese, Los Angeles: Red Granite Pictures, 2013.

I'm **not** the kind of person who will tell you what you want to hear. I'd much rather tell you what you **need to know**.

I'm a terrible salesperson, but I am a good teacher. I am lucky enough to be able to talk about money in terms that most people can understand.

So, if you're ready to look ahead into a financial future that you participate in, understand, and are comfortable with—then forget everything you've wanted to hear. I'm going to tell you what you need to know.

The same holds true for this book. It won't be too complicated to understand.

In the pages to come I will teach you how to understand your money a little more using simple, everyday language. I can do that not because I'm exceptionally smart, but because I dedicate my life to learning all that I can about investing safely for retirement—the good, the bad, and the ugly.

When I hear about a new type of investment, I don't always understand it right away. I need to find out more about it. I want to know what the pros and cons are. I ask the questions that many others want to ask, but may not be able to, or may be afraid to ask: the common-sense questions that break down the barriers between "finance guys" and you and me.

I approach every new offering as if I'm going to invest in it, so I know that if I offer it to you, I know it inside out and can explain it to you in a way that you understand.

If you're looking for an honest, straightforward, and clear perspective on what your options are for investing and saving, and, as we'll cover, how those two are not the same thing, then I *know* you'll be happy that you picked up this book.

My aim in writing this is simple: I want you to walk into your financial life every day with more confidence that you may have a better understanding of your money.

In the coming pages, we'll go over common myths in the market and who you can work with to manage your money. I will outline what types of investment options there are, the upsides and downsides of each one, and the connection between investing and taxes—all in a language that is easy to understand.

Read on, and I will help you understand your money better—the ins and outs of what your money can do.

Chapter 1

MYTHS AND MISCONCEPTIONS OF THE MARKET

Our brains are powerful, and we've evolved to recognize patterns so that we can repeat them—"monkey see, monkey do," as they say. Drive a certain way to work every morning, and after a while, you'll start operating on cruise control. You'll get to work and not really remember how you got there—you knew the way without seeming to make any conscious decisions.

Have you ever changed residence and after work you started driving to your old home?

Our brains want to grasp onto patterns, giving us shortcuts to operate more efficiently so that we can save

1

our energy for other processes. However, our strong pattern recognition skills leave us vulnerable to conditioning.

Hear a rumor enough times and soon your brain considers it fact. This leads to misconceptions and makes it hard for us to recognize and acknowledge mistakes.

For example, you know the most famous line from *The Empire Strikes Back*?[3]

"Luke, I am your father."

It tops many famous movie quote lists, and it has become completely ingrained in our culture.

Darth Vader never actually says that in the movie.

He really says, "***No***, I am your father."

You may remember him saying it the other way—most of us do. This is because we've heard or seen it referenced so many times by people that we know, people on TV, in books, articles, etc. But go back and watch the clip from the movie, and you'll see the real line.

Our brains latch on to "common knowledge," accepting it as true so that we can focus on more pressing things. This can be helpful for some things, such as remembering the directions to work, but it can also cause problems, as we don't recognize or question basic mistakes we've made, because we think we know the way.

I am not trying to drive people crazy or to make them feel any less smart. I share this with you to convey how easily our

---

3   *Star Wars: Episode V – The Empire Strikes Back*, directed by Irvin Kershner, USA: Lucasfilm, 1980.

brains can grasp onto patterns, associations, and hearsay; how easily we can believe fiction to be fact.

Our minds are predisposed to accept myths and misconceptions, especially if they are repeated to us. It's important to recognize this before you read what I am going to tell you.

Just because you've heard something before, even if you've heard it a hundred or a thousand times, **does not mean that it's true**.

Sometimes we hear something about an investment that is not true, but we hear it so often that we think, *Of course that must be true, it's common knowledge!*

Be careful about what you read on the internet, too. Not everything online is accurate. I pay very close attention to where information is coming from and to make sure that I understand *why* something would be true, rather than accepting that what I read is true just because it was published.

To properly save for retirement, you need to know the upsides and the downsides of most every common investment in my opinion. Once you know the facts, then you can make good decisions.

I can't predict the future, and I certainly can't predict the market, but I can help you become a more informed investor.

To start with, we're going to counter some common myths and misconceptions in the market.

These myths below are very, very common. When you see them, you may think they are true. I encourage you to keep an open mind.

If something sounds true to you, think about why that might be. Is it because what you've been told is based on a good explanation? Or have you heard it so many times, perhaps from people that you trust, that you've accepted that it must be true? Perhaps you may even *want* to believe some of these myths to be true—if they are, it's good news for you!

Unfortunately, whether it is good for you has no bearing on whether it is true. So, I'm going to tell you what you need to know—even if it's not what you want to hear.

Myth #1: "A balanced portfolio is a diversified portfolio."

One of the major misconceptions in the financial industry is about diversification. Diversification means that your money is spread among a variety of *different* things.

Typically, when the market goes down and clients lose value in their portfolios, their financial professional may respond by telling clients that they need to "rebalance their portfolio to **diversify** more to minimize their risk of loss." That's music to the clients' ears, and they continue to associate "rebalancing" with "diversifying" and a lack of risk.

However, let's look at this more closely.

There's no doubt that diversity—having a range of *different* things in your portfolio—can help you minimize loss in the event of a market correction. But what does diversity mean?

When a financial professional diversifies your portfolio by, say, moving you out of certain stock funds and into bond funds, it's true that your portfolio will *look* a little different.

You may feel some relief because you've heard that bonds are safer than stocks, and the deeply ingrained associations between "bonds" and "safe" will make you feel good. If you're "diversified," then you can't possibly lose money . . . right?

Well, no. While traditional bonds may be safer than stocks, the traditional bond portfolio idea has gone by the wayside because lenders can't do it as much anymore—bonds don't pay what they used to.

Today's rebalanced portfolios don't hold that many traditional bonds. Instead, financial professionals will move clients toward what they call *bond funds*, which sound similar, but are quite different from traditional bonds. Financial professionals may also call these bond funds **fixed income funds**. It's rare to see them called what they really are—**bond mutual funds**.

Like traditional bonds, if bond funds go up with the market, you most likely won't receive as much gain as you would with a stock fund.

However, when the market goes down, bond funds are very different from bonds. While many traditional bonds are guaranteed regardless of market performance if held to maturity, bond funds simply may not *lose as much* as stocks in the event of a downward market correction. Key words: "As much."

You can still lose money with bond funds. In fact, during certain market corrections, many bond funds **lost more than 30 percent**.[4] That's a big loss for a product that is supposed to be "secure," particularly if you are in or nearing retirement.

On top of that, bond funds often have a fee attached, which means that whether you make money or lose it, the financial professional and the manager of the fund both get paid out of your money.

If you have bond funds, you may not even be aware of these fees. Wall Street has done an incredible job of hiding their fees on your statements by taking them right out of the returns and embedding them directly into losses without differentiating for clients between market performance and their fees.

Bond funds have lower upside, they *do* have downside, and they have fees attached. How is that different from the stocks or mutual funds that you were just in?

While a financial professional may put you in bond funds and say that your money is "diversified," I don't consider a diversified portfolio in the market to be a balanced portfolio— your money is still 100 percent *in the market*.

---

4   Nathan Hale, "Oppenheimer's Bond-Fund Blowup: Worse Than You Think," *CBS MoneyWatch*, April 20, 2009, http://www.cbsnews.com/news/oppenheimers-bond-fund-blowup-worse-than-you-think/.

All of it is in *one* type of money—at risk. You can buy stock in two different companies, or buy two different mutual funds, but they're in the same category of risk; you can lose money in all of them, so it's not *truly* diversified. All your money is in one thing (the market) and not a range of things (balanced).

Of course, financial professionals want you in the market—that's how they make their living. But if you have all your money in the market, there's no amount of diversification you can do within the market that will make your portfolio truly balanced, because it is all at risk.

I believe in *true* diversification. To truly diversify your money, you can't risk all of it. You should have a balanced portfolio in the market, but you may want to have other ***types*** of assets that **aren't tied to market performance**. My version of diversification includes both at-risk and risk-free investments.

Myth #2: "It's never a bad time to buy!"

"Buy low, sell high! Buy high, sell higher!"

These are some of the refrains that you'll hear from financial professionals and the financial media, who are eager to capitalize on the average investor's fear of missing out.

Fear of missing out is a powerful motivator, but it rarely leads to good investments. In fact, some of the best decisions we make involve going in the opposite direction of everyone else. But that rational path often clashes with the powerful emotional fear of missing out.

When the market is low, financial professionals will tell you, "It's a great time to buy, buy, and buy! Sell when it's high!"

When the market is high (the time they had told you that you should sell), those very same financial professionals encourage you to hold, because "bigger gains are just around the corner!"

But let's examine their own adage: "Buy low, sell *high*."

So, following their claim, you *should* sell at a high point.

Well, financial professionals may want to keep you in the market even when you are at a high point, because that's how they earn their living. If you are up, it's emotionally hard to sell, the fear of missing out—which is no small fear, especially if you bought a hot stock when it was low—may tempt you with the allure of bigger gains to come.

So, they'll keep you in, even if you reach the "high" point of the "buy low, sell high" pitch. Then, when bigger gains don't come, and the market corrects downward, you'll never hear financial professionals tell you to sell. At that point, the market is down again—so it's a great time to buy more!

"Buy and hold," they'll say. "That's our strategy."

So, when *should* you sell?

For many financial professionals, the answer just may be simple:

Never.

Remember Mark Hanna, Matthew McConaughey's character from *The Wolf of Wall Street*?[5] Here's what he said to Jordan Belfort (DiCaprio) in a scene discussing this subject:

"If you've got a client who bought a stock at eight, and now it sits at sixteen, and he's all happy and he wants to get out, you don't let him do that."

A surprised young Belfort struggles to absorb this, and Hanna asks:

"What do you do?"

Belfort squirms in silence—he doesn't know.

Hanna answers his own question, "You have another brilliant idea for a stock for him to reinvest . . . Then you keep doing this, repeatedly, and again. Meanwhile, he thinks he's getting rich, which he is, *on paper*. But you and me, *the brokers,* are taking home **cold hard cash** via commission."

Hanna leans back in his chair, proud to have delivered this insight to the young Belfort. Belfort then replies, "That's incredible. I can't tell you how excited I am."

The goal for the financial professional is to keep your assets under management. To accomplish this, they have conditioned us to feel good about strategies that at face value aren't sound, such as "It's never a bad time to buy!"

I do believe that the market will often recover from losses, but that doesn't mean it's always a good time to buy. The key is—how long will it take for the market to rebound to the point where we'll see new money?

---

5   *Wolf of Wall Street*, Scorsese, 2013.

It is not a smart financial strategy to have to wait six to eight years and perhaps longer to get back to where we were. In fact, even if we do recover to square one in a decade, we are not even back to where we were, because of inflation—$100,000 doesn't have as much purchasing power today as it did ten years ago.

Despite all of this, conditioning works—I can't even count the number of times that intelligent people—really, truly smart people—have smiled as they've told me, "I'm back to where I was," as if it were an enormous achievement. I'd be wearing an angry face.

It's scary to think that we can be conditioned to be happy with a financial strategy of waiting so many years just to return to (almost) where we started.

Or, as Hanna describes it in the movie, "Keep the clients on the Ferris wheel . . . and that's how it goes, every day, every decade, every century."

Financial professionals will encourage you when you're experiencing losses, calling your vanished money, "merely paper losses." However, you never hear them call your market gains "merely paper gains."

Here's the thing: These ideas of lows and highs are entirely artificial—*no one can predict what "low" or "high" will really mean.* If we're at a historically high point, there's no guarantee that the market won't go higher, just as there's no guarantee that it *will*. The same holds true for low points, as the Great Depression and the Great Recession showed us.

In that same scene from *The Wolf of Wall Street*, Hanna tells Belfort, "Nobody, whether you're Warren Buffett or Jimmy Buffett, knows if a stock is going to go up or down, *least of all* stock brokers." But that won't stop financial professionals from making recommendations.

Myth #3: "My Financial professional has my best interests at heart."

Not every financial professional is a Madoff in waiting, trying to defraud you out of your hard-earned retirement money. There are some, but we're not focusing on them here. The reason this statement is a myth has more to do with the nature of the financial industry than any one person's ethics.

Even the most well-intentioned financial professional is operating in a system that is never completely aligned with your best interests. While financial professionals may call themselves financial advisors or retirement planners, that isn't exactly accurate. Many in fact are employees at a store. In their case, the store is a bank or financial institution. Their job is to sell the products from that store. Nothing wrong with that. I just prefer to give my clients more options than just one company I work for.

That's the entire purpose of their profession.

They're not going to tell you that maybe you should try something different, like a staggered approach to CDs, or real estate, or fixed annuities. The selection at their store is stocks and other funds in the market; if you walk in the door, they expect that you're looking for what they're selling. You shouldn't expect to buy anything else from them. Just as you wouldn't walk into a flower shop and expect to buy lawn furniture.

A financial professional that is captive with a company may offer the best plans available for that company. It is their job to sell financial products to **make money for the company**.

Myth #4: "My financial professional is personally considering my portfolio on an individual basis and rebalancing as necessary, so I can understand paying high fees."

Most financial professionals categorize individual investors by risk assessments and choose investments for them from a selection of existing funds that fit into those risk categories. To the financial professionals, these funds generally look like different pie charts of stock and bond funds—some are labeled "conservative," others are "moderate," and some are "aggressive."

Your financial professionals will likely allocate your investment account into the pie chart that most closely resembles your risk profile. Typically, the older you are, the more conservative your funds will be. While it is true that these funds are managed, your financial professional is usually not personally managing them.

Myth #5: "The fees aren't that high— isn't it only 1 percent of my portfolio?"

Financial professionals talk about fees as if they are normal.

"I've got to charge a fee. After all, the better you do, the better I'll do, blah, blah, blah."

They condition you to expect fees, to think there is no other option, and that fees are no big deal. However, it is important to understand all the fees that you're paying and their impact, even if your financial professional says it's "just 1 percent."

While 1 percent doesn't sound high, that number can significantly gouge your market returns. John C. Bogle, the founder of Vanguard Investment Group (one of the biggest investment management groups in the world), said that because of the "compounding expenses" of fees, **fund owners receive only about 30 percent of the market returns**, while the **"purveyors of the services"** (those charging the fees) *receive about 70 percent of the market returns.*[6]

Now **that** sounds significant, right?

Have you ever heard a financial professional tell you that you may be giving up 70 percent of the market returns due to their fees?

Financial professionals may want to make you feel good about what they're selling. Selling you on paying fees

---

6   Jason M. Breslow, "John Bogle: 'The Train Wreck' Awaiting American Retirement," *PBS*, April 23, 2013, http://www.pbs. org/wgbh/frontline/article/john-bogle-the-train-wreck-awaiting-american-retirement/.

by minimizing them as "only 1 percent" sounds a lot better than telling you that you may be giving up 70 percent of the market's returns.

Myth #6: "If I put all of my money in the market, I can expect a 10 percent return."

We have all heard this. You can expect an *average* return of 10 percent on your investments. While it is true that in any given year, a market-based portfolio *can* experience a 10 percent rate of return (certainly higher than a savings account will), to call this an "average" is misleading.

To be able to calculate an "average" return of 10 percent, you may need to include market statistics dating so far back, to the 1800s—statistics that don't have much bearing on today's financial or economic climate.

Today, an average rate of return of 3 percent to 6 percent may be a more reasonable expectation. Keep in mind that any return a financial professional advertises is an *expectation*, since he cannot guarantee a return of any amount.

However, even if a financial professional *could* say that you can expect a 10 percent average rate of return, that doesn't necessarily mean that you'll earn anything significant.

For example, let's say they put you into an aggressive fund that has an incredible year, with a return of 100 percent. **Your money doubles**, say from $100,000 to $200,000. The next year the fund cools off and drops by 50 percent. You should still have done well, right?

Well, no.

When your $200,000 goes down by 50 percent, it is now back to $100,000.

So, let's do the math (not too much, I promise):

$100,000 100 percent = $200,000 50 percent $100,000

100 percent 50 percent = 50 percent 2 (amount of years) 25 percent average rate of return.

You didn't earn a penny in the two years, but the financial professional and money manager can boast that the fund yielded an average rate of return of 25 percent.

Imagine the fee they could justify for a fund that returns an average of 25 percent!

Myth #7: "All annuities are the same, and all annuities are bad."

Investment products—annuities included—are complicated. Saying that you dislike annuities is like saying that you dislike cars. There are so many cars to choose from. Some cars are good, some are bad. Similarly, there are a variety of annuities. Some annuities are good, some are not. To say all annuities are bad is well, unknowledgeable to say the least.

When you hear "all annuities are bad," it may be wise to consider the source. Many financial professionals are not licensed to offer fixed-indexed annuities, so they can't make money from them. In fact, many financial professionals lose money under management when their clients choose to purchase fixed-indexed annuities with funds that they had previously invested with the financial professional.

So, for some so-called financial professionals, their statement is true; all annuities *are* bad. But *your* interests are different than theirs, and certain annuities may well be good for you. When a financial professional says that all annuities are bad, could they be looking out for their interests and not yours?

Myth #8: "Everyone loses money at some point; the market will always come back up."

Financial professionals often tell you that everyone loses money and that it will come back. Have you ever heard the following from them?

"Well, you only lost X; others have lost twice as much!"

As if we should be comforted that we didn't lose as much as their other customers. For all we know, they are using us as an example to others, telling them, "At least you didn't lose as much as this guy!"

Your financial professional can talk all day about historic rates of return and console you after losses by telling you that it happens to everyone and that the market will go up. I agree that in most cases, the market will correct and continue to rise. But no one can predict *when* the market will go up or down.

If you're young, you have time on your side to recuperate from losses. But if, for example, you were in or near retirement when the Great Recession hit, you know in a gut-wrenching way just how hard those losses are to swallow.

Here's the key: Just because the market is likely to come back up doesn't mean that *you* will benefit from it. If you are nearing retirement, then you are at the mercy of timing and of a market that no one can predict. Maybe you'll recover, and maybe, like many people in the last decade, you won't.

The unpredictability of the market reminds me of a few years back, when I visited a friend of mine in the hospital. It was the end of a long day of work, and I had skipped lunch that day; even though dinner was waiting for me at home, I wanted to check in on my friend first.

After a couple of hours chatting with him, I was ravenous, and as you know, hospitals weren't exactly full of quality food, although they are much better today. Searching for a snack, I wandered into a hallway with a lone vending machine.

I put a dollar in the machine and typed on the keypad for a package of cookies. I watched the coil with the cookies spin around and around, and then get caught.

No cookies fell my way.

I didn't mind putting in another dollar to get my cookies. I figured that it was better this way—now I could have two packages of cookies with the added alibi, "I had no choice."

Dollar in, buttons pressed, coils spinning.

Cookies caught again.

Two packages of cookies hung, just out of reach. I was out two dollars, with no cookies to show for it, and no more cash to spend.

I pushed the machine, hoping to rattle the cookies free. No luck—they bolt those machines.

I thought that I was going to bust my shoulder trying to make the machine move, but those cookies stayed put. Not eager to spend the night in the hospital with a busted shoulder, I let it go, thinking, "Boy, do I hate losing money!"

I drove home hungry, had dinner, and then got into bed, but I had trouble sleeping that night. I was still upset about losing money in the vending machine. I opened my eyes and my little red alarm clock said 11:10.

I remember thinking: "Somebody is going to put a dollar in and get *three packages of cookies.*" If it hadn't been for my wife, I probably would have jumped in the car with some more money and gone back to claim the cookies.

Overall, it wasn't a big deal, but that night stayed with me because it reminds me so much of market timing. Some financial professionals can condition us every day to be okay with losing money, like it's nothing.

We can open our statements and see that we're down thousands or tens of thousands of dollars.

When you get him on the phone, he will urge you to "come in, and we'll diversify your portfolio some more." He'll tell you not to worry, to "just hold on. It'll come back. It's only a paper loss."

While the market probably will go up again, nobody knows when, or how much. This may not be as important to the financial professionals, who gets paid either way, but it's huge for you.

The American dream is not to have your life savings raided by a market correction, and to have to wait eight, nine, or ten years, hoping just to regain the money that your retirement accounts lost.

It doesn't matter to you if the next person comes along and gets three packages of cookies for one dollar. If you only had two dollars to spend and they got eaten up by a market correction, you're going hungry.

Myth #9: "If you lose money, I lose money."

I hear this one all the time. Clients say their financial professional told them, "Hey, if you lose money, I lose money." I say, boy, they need to get the dictionary out.

There's a big difference between **losing** money and *making less* money. Let's say you have a portfolio of $100,000 and you're paying 2 percent in fees. In that case, your financial professional charges $2,000 a year for managing your portfolio.

But if the market has a minor correction of 20 percent, now you have $80,000. **You lost $20,000**.

Did your financial professional lose any money? Let's look. You still must pay their fee even though you lost money. So, while you lost $20,000, your financial professional *made* $1,600 for himself and his company.

You are **down** $20,000, and he's **up** $1,600.

They didn't lose money. **They made money.**

Sure, they're *making less than they would have* if the market had gone up, but you lost money—that's very different.

Wouldn't you switch with them all day long?

Imagine that instead of the way it is now, that when the market goes down, **you** make less, but *they* lose money. How much money do you think they'd have to lose before they fired you as a client?

(Answer: Not much.)

Here's the crazy part—when we lose tens of thousands of dollars in an investment, who is the first person we call for the solution? The person who lost us the money. We think that the person who caused the problem can fix it.

Now if that isn't a misconception, I don't know what is.

They already know what they're going to say when you call them after a loss: "Why don't you come in, we have to diversify you a little bit more."

Sound familiar?

We're back to myth number one ("a balanced portfolio is a diversified portfolio"), and the cycle continues, every day, every decade, every century.

The financial industry isn't designed to make things clear to the average investor, just as a flower shop isn't interested in talking with you about lawn furniture.

I'm not trying to say that the people working in the financial industry are sinister—I'm part of this industry, after all, and I try to be as transparent as possible.

I am saying the industry is very different than it seems at first glance, and there is a ton of misinformation out there that has become so ingrained in us that we believe it is true.

Unfortunately, we, as humans, fear what we don't understand, the media prey on our fears, and many investment firms don't educate us—they ask us to trust them blindly and pay them for the pleasure.

So, what should the average investor do? What is the solution to help keep you afloat and on course in the choppy seas of the market, the media, and the companies that push products all day long?

By reading this book, you're on the right track. You're taking charge of your money by setting yourself up to understand the realities of investing, which will help you make more informed decisions.

Now that you've seen the truth behind common myths about the market and learned that the things you've heard repeatedly may not be true, it may seem hard to trust anyone.

You should trust some people, but as with anything else, think critically about it, ask questions, and **get answers that work for you** before trusting someone with your money. I like to share with my clients all the pros and cons of their investment options so that they can understand and decide for themselves which ones are right for them.

In the next chapter, we'll go over the various types of people who can help you.

Chapter 2

WHO'S WHO IN
THE FINANCIAL WORLD?

don't think it's a question of whether you should invest. I'm assuming if you are reading this book, then you are ready to start investing or that you are already an investor.

The real question is: Whom do you work with for your investments?

Depending on your goals, you may need two or three different investment people. On the other hand, having one person manage all your investments may simplify your financial life. Whether you're working with one or several people, whom you choose is an important decision.

There are various aspects to money management that you need to consider. You may value safety; you may want your money to grow; and I'll bet you want to be able to withdraw your money one day and keep as much of it as you can, instead of giving it all to Uncle Sam.

There are several types of people who can help you with your money, so we'll go over each of them here and lay out what they can and cannot do for you.

————————

There are basically three types of financial advisors, and each one can offer you different things.

Before we look at the types of investments available to you, let's investigate the types of financial professionals who can help you.

Types of Financial Professionals

The three most common types of financial professionals are:

- Brokers
- Insurance Agents
- Investment Advisor Representatives (IARs)

Brokers

What are brokers?

Brokers are licensed in most cases to sell securities in the market, such as stocks, bond funds, mutual funds, variable annuities, and other products. Many brokers work for companies that sell some of these products. Some may be independent.

What do brokers offer?

Brokers sell investment products that are "in the market" per what their company offers, earning a commission. This may include any combination of stocks, bond funds, mutual funds, variable annuities, etc.

Do brokers give tax advice?

Rarely. In many cases, it's not that brokers *can't* give tax advice; it's that their employers do not allow them to do so.

I have seen many people coming up on retirement with all their assets at risk in the market, yet they claim that their priority is keeping their money safe. In most of these situations, it turns out that they're working with brokers to find safer investments. Remember, the broker's job is to put them in the market, which at times is inherently unsafe; he can't take them out of it.

Many of these people think their money is safe because their broker told them they have low-risk investment portfolios. From the broker's perspective, he is keeping the client's funds *as safe as he can* within the product line that he can sell.

Insurance Agents

What are insurance agents?

Insurance agents are licensed to sell fixed annuities, fixed-indexed annuities, life insurance, long-term care insurance, and health insurance.

There are two types of insurance agents: agents who work for a company and independent agents who work for themselves, such as myself.

Captive agents work specifically with one company.

Independent agents are free to "shop" around and offer insurance products from many companies.

I started my career as a captive agent working for a specific company. I quickly learned that my hands were tied because I could not offer products from outside companies, even if I knew that another company had a better option for my clients' needs.

That didn't sit right with me, which is why I am 100 percent independent. I work for myself, which in turn means I work for my clients, not a company.

I haven't been handcuffed to a single company for more than fifteen years, and I'm thrilled to be able to offer my clients the best options available in the industry!

What do insurance agents offer?

Insurance agents offer insurance products such as life insurance, health insurance, long-term care insurance, fixed annuities, and fixed-indexed annuities among other things.

Do insurance agents give tax advice?

Rarely. In many cases it's not that insurance agents *can't* give tax advice, it's that their employers do not allow them to do so.

Investment Advisor Representatives (IARs)

What are investment advisor representatives?

An investment advisor representative (IAR) refers to a person registered with the Securities and Exchange Commission (SEC) and/or a state's securities agency. Investment advisor representatives work for registered investment advisory firms (RIAs), such as my company.

What do investment advisor representatives offer?

Investment advisor representatives offer products in the market, including stocks, bonds, exchange-traded funds (ETFs) and mutual funds among other things. For products in the market, investment advisor representatives charge a management fee and have a fiduciary responsibility to put their clients' needs above their own interests and above those of any company.

Do investment advisor representatives give tax advice?

Yes, they can.

Have you ever had a financial professional ask you to move with him or her to a new company? Then when you did move, they wanted to reposition your assets into the new company's financial strategies?

It's certainly fair to wonder what happened to the old company's great products and strategies that the financial professional had sold you over the years.

Were they **all** suddenly no good for you?

Maybe you can take the question a step further—were they ever really invested in the financial strategy of the old company? Fair to ask, because they sold us on the company. Or was it just a paycheck, and now he's on to the next paycheck from a new company?

The sudden change in your investment products brings up another, even more important question: Whose interests are being served here? Yours, or theirs?

Companies and professionals seeking to sell their own products will steer clients away from other products as much as possible so that they can make money. It's gotten so bad now that I see many financial professionals tell people they offer things that they really don't.

A nice lady and her husband came to my educational seminar and afterwards made an appointment with me. She was sixty-five years old, a widow of about five years who had recently remarried. The newlyweds came to the appointment together. Although they kept their finances separate, they each knew each other's general financial positions. She had been working with the same financial professional for about thirteen years at the time, and she told me that he was great, and he had become a friend.

Truth be told, I believed her; he probably was great at what he does—selling his company's products. But his hands were still tied to offer only what his company allowed him to offer to his clients—friends or not.

She told me, "At this point in my life, I want to keep what I have. I don't want to lose anything. I just want to earn a few bucks to keep up with inflation."

She brought in an investment statement so that I could look at her account. I was flabbergasted when I saw it.

Even though she was sixty-five, she was invested as aggressively as I would expect if she were thirty-five. She'd been invested nearly the same way for the past thirteen years, with only a few small adjustments.

I told her, "Your risk is too high."

Surprised, she replied, "I told my broker I wanted to be ultra-safe."

I recommended a fixed-indexed annuity to her, and she said, "You know, Doug, I've heard about that, it sounds great. My new husband has a fixed-indexed annuity and has been very happy, but I asked the guy my late husband and I have been working with, and he told me, 'If I thought you needed an annuity, I would have offered it to you.'"

I knew what I knew and, of course, you only know what you know, but *she* didn't know what I knew. She had also been working with this broker for more than thirteen years—she saw him as a friend.

I said, "I have an idea. Do you want to have a little investigative fun?"

"What do you mean?" She asked.

"I'm going to call your broker house on speaker phone." I said. "Not your broker," I assured her, "just the company."

I called and asked the gentleman on the phone if they offered fixed-indexed annuities.

"No, we don't." He said quickly, without having to think about it.

She looked puzzled; her broker had told her that he would have offered it to her if he thought she needed it. She didn't know what to make of this new information.

Still on the phone, I asked the rep from the broker house:

"I'm am an investment advisor representative. If I came to work for your company, I understand you guys sell mutual funds, mutual bond funds, stocks, variable annuities . . . But what if I have a client who wants a fixed-indexed annuity, so she can protect her principal and earn a decent rate of return? Can I offer that to her?"

The rep on the phone didn't know the answer offhand, so he placed me on hold for a while. Finally, a new person came on the phone—at this point they wanted me to come in for an interview to work for them.

I pressed, "I just need to know this."

The man finally informed me, "No, you can't."

"What would happen if I did offer the client a fixed-indexed annuity?" I asked.

"We'd terminate your contract," he told me. We call that selling away.

I said, "My God, that's not in the client's best interest."

The lady in my office was shocked. She felt hurt, betrayed even, by her broker. But unfortunately, because of the nature of his position, his hands were tied.

Her broker couldn't offer a fixed-indexed annuity because doing so would be "selling away." By offering her an annuity, he would be taking money away from the products his employer charges fees on and thus directly competing with his employer. As a business, they don't want that, so many do not allow their employees to do it.

I can look at what they're selling and say, "This isn't in my client's best interest. I can't offer this to them." These companies don't want to hire employees who need to put the client's interests above the company's sales goals.

I believe that as an industry, we must get away from the "selling" mentality. A big reason I'm writing this book is that I'm concerned about many people being told things that aren't true about investing, and as a result, not really understanding the investments they have.

Typically, when I feel that someone is a good candidate for a product I like, such as a fixed-indexed annuity, that person must take money away from his or her financial professional to purchase the annuity. That's a loss for the financial professional, even if it will benefit the client. A lot of times, financial professionals will give misinformation to their clients to keep them.

That's not how I want to do business.

I seek to provide value by educating people on all their options and helping them meet their goals. I'm not going to try to steer a client away from something or give them a product that may not be right for them just because I can sell it.

I value the fact that if someone comes into my office with a good investment portfolio for them, then I'll tell her to keep it—I've done that many times. If the portfolio is not good, then I'll give that client a solution, too.

It's up to the clients at that point; I merely educate them. I don't talk people into doing anything. My money is already secure. I recommend what I think they should do, based on helping them with their individual needs and not based on a personal goal to get assets under management.

Beware of financial professionals who give vague answers

I've heard countless stories over the years from clients about vague answers they've received from financial professionals.

I've encountered the same confusing and misleading answers repeatedly in my career, often in conjunction with catchy sales pitches for investment products that had *major* cons lurking just beneath the surface.

Many times, clients get vague answers from financial professionals when they ask what they're paying in fees. Financial professionals often give a roundabout answer to that question. "Around 1 percent," for example, without specifying 1 percent of *what*. Or they'll try to brush off the question by saying, "It doesn't matter what you must pay, it matters what you keep."

A lot of people will accept that.

I don't.

At my seminars, I always ask, "Would you let your kids get away with that?" Imagine that your kid comes home, and you ask him, "What did you get on your test?"

If your child replied, "I passed. What does it matter what I got?" would that be all right with you?

We don't let our kids get away with the stuff we let the people managing our life savings get away with. If a person can't give you good, specific answers that allow **you** to understand what's happening with your money, beware.

Taxes and tax professionals

Regardless of how you invest, you must file taxes. Many people use tax preparers for that purpose. There are also tax strategists. It's important not to confuse the two.

I often hear people say, "I'm going to talk to my CPA about an investment." The problem is that most CPAs don't specialize in investments; they handle tax preparation. What are CPAs supposed to say when you ask them about an investment?

Their job is to take what you give them—your W-2 forms, 1099s, investment statements, and so forth—and put the numbers into the appropriate boxes to determine your tax liability. That's tax preparation.

Tax strategy (or tax planning) is looking at your taxes and adjusting so that you're following the laws, to lower your tax liability if possible.

To make the best financial decisions, you need somebody who can advise you on investments *and* somebody who can advise you on tax strategy. Whether those are the same person or different people, you need both of those functions, and ideally the two should communicate with each other.

Many investors do have both investment advisors and tax advisors. However, the two usually don't talk to each other, which can cause major problems.

I recognized this early on in my career, so I learned how to give not only investment advice but tax advice too, so that I could provide the best possible service to clients. At my company, I help clients with tax planning as part of our service.

Many financial professionals don't do this. If you have a financial professional, look at the bottom of your statement. It will usually say something to the effect of "Don't ask us for tax advice. We are not tax people. Go to your tax person for advice on your taxes."

Most companies have policies that do not allow their financial professionals to give tax advice. As a result, I've seen financial professionals make recommendations that are tax-heavy when they don't need to be, which can be disastrous.

Who cares if you earn a thousand dollars if you must pay six hundred dollars in taxes?

I don't understand how someone can give investment advice without taking taxes into account, yet many people do—at times, to the client's detriment.

Because I give investment *and* tax advice, oftentimes what I recommend is based on the client's tax situation. We go over their needs and come up with the best way to accomplish their goals. Sometimes simply adjusting when they take money out—even by just a few weeks—can help them keep more of their money.

Smart tax planning is also vital when it comes to distributing money in retirement, because the tax implications of which accounts one withdraws from and when makes a huge difference in how much of their money they keep.

Many times, we can do things to get retirement money out of a taxable situation at a discounted tax rate. This is very important to consider when investing—ultimately the amount you keep is what matters, not what you earn "on paper."

At age seventy-three, most people must start withdrawing money from many (but not all) retirement accounts. However, that doesn't mean you must wait until then. Several of my clients have saved money on taxes by withdrawing money from retirement accounts before they were required to, then reinvesting those withdrawals into tax-friendlier and sometimes tax-free solutions.

Some people retire early and are in extremely low tax brackets for a very short time before Social Security, pensions, and other required minimum distributions kick in.

Say they have an IRA, which means they must pay taxes on withdrawals. By taking some money out of their IRA while they are in a low tax bracket and moving it to a Roth IRA (which features tax-free withdrawals), they can potentially save money on taxes now *and* later.

They may pay fewer taxes on their IRA withdrawals now and take tax-free distributions from their Roth IRA later without increasing the taxes on their other income, which means they may be able to keep more money overall.

That's tax strategy, and a great example of why your investment advisors and tax professionals should work closely together, in my opinion. If people are giving you advice about how much money you can make, they should be able to help you keep as much of it as possible.

What I believe

- **Legal obligations:** We must be fully compliant with the American Federal Trade Commission Act, which sets out the legal framework for protecting confidential non-public personal data.

- **Contractual duties:** Every agreement or contract that we enter implies duties and obligations, which we shall fulfill at the highest level of professionalism.

- **Professional secrecy:** We are bound by professional secrecy, as an American fiduciary, to protect clients' confidentiality at its highest level.

For us, putting our clients first is about more than just our legal responsibility. We care about our clients as people, not just as customers.

People helping people: A way of life that my mother taught me

The idea of putting people first was ingrained in me from a young age. My mom had a motto that she imparted to me: "**People helping people.**" I love those words and I love the meaning. She meant that if you can help someone, it is an **honor and a privilege that should be cherished**, never a burden. It is a pleasure to be of service to people who need it.

My parents ran a hotel and restaurant when I was growing up, and I was always amazed at how much they helped people out. When times were tough, they let guests stay at the hotel even if they were short on the bill. Our guests would often use their skills to help us out in return, such as trimming the bushes or doing the dishes.

The neat thing about people helping people is that it is contagious, and it leads to a better life and society.

For me, *people helping people* applies to each of our own unique skills to help others. We all have strengths and weaknesses, and by trying to simply help others with our knowledge and expertise, we can make an impact. For me, of course, that includes my professional knowledge and skills related to investing, but it extends beyond that.

For example, my neighbor's fence once broke while he was out of town for a lengthy trip, so I fixed it for him. I could help, so I did. It's as simple as that—people helping people.

The amazing thing is, my mother's motto runs forward and back; "people" are on either side of "helping," which is apt, because helping others often inspires them to do the same for you.

At my parents' hotel, one guest fixed a shower floor for us without asking for anything. He was a construction worker, and he noticed a crack in the floor. He pulled out the floor, put in new floorboards, and sealed everything. He told my mother about the problem only after he had fixed it. He simply saw a problem he could solve, so he decided to help.

My parents were so focused on helping people that it inspired the helping spirit in others. I have benefited so much from adopting that mindset and applying it to my life—in business and beyond.

If I can help people, even outside of their finances, I am happy to do it. Helping people is rewarding for me. I live for moments when I can make a positive impact on someone's life.

And just as caring for people inspired others to help my mother, I have been fortunate enough to receive help from many great people as well. By using my knowledge on retirement investing and my other skills to help people, I have formed many relationships with great people who in turn were kind enough to allow me to lean on their expertise in other areas when I've needed it.

When my mom was sick, I called upon the knowledge of several of my clients who were nurses and doctors. They understood my mom's condition and the medical lingo surrounding her treatment that I was unfamiliar with, so they helped me understand how best to care for her. They were happy to help, and I am grateful for their guidance. I hope that I can return the favor whenever they need some support that I can provide.

It all comes back to **"people helping people"** as mom would say.

At work, I believe that my job is to alleviate clients' worries, especially when it comes to keeping their hard-earned money secure. If I can find a way to help my clients, I *enjoy* doing it.

People helping people!

My company: A one-stop shop for retirement investing and tax advice

I created our office to help people in as many financial areas as possible, all in one place, including providing investment advice for products in the market, insurance products, and tax advice. Kind of a one-stop shop, if you will.

A lot of companies don't want to take on the liability of offering investment *and* tax advice. We welcome it because we believe it is the way to do the best job for the client.

I have mentors because I make sure to surround myself with great people so that I can offer my clients the best!

The return gained from working with us shows up in more than just a client's investment statements.

I've always felt that your investment advisors and tax advisors should talk, and financial advisors should be able to look at a tax return and understand it, which is rarer than you'd think in this business.

I have seen many people pay too much in taxes because their financial professional and tax preparer don't talk to each other. In many cases, the issue is not the tax preparer, who is simply determining the client's tax liability based on their investments, income, deductions, and so forth. The real problem may be that a financial professional put the client into investments without paying attention to his or her tax situation.

I can look at clients' tax returns and sometimes save them some money on taxes by adjusting the way they're invested. We have been able to review new clients' tax returns and find ways to lower their tax liability by thousands of dollars from one year to the next. That's a real and immediate return that came from our ability to advise on investments *and* provide tax strategy.

If your investment advisors don't have the knowledge and ability to execute tax strategy, or they don't collaborate with tax professionals, then I don't see how they can provide the best possible service.

It's important to have every part of your financial management team in communication with each other and working together. That's why I created my company, and that's what we do today.

Whom you should work with: More than just a title

The types of investments a person helps you with certainly plays into whom you should work with, but there is more to it than that. There are good and bad financial professionals in each category, and chemistry between you and the person managing your money is important.

Whether you're looking for a broker, investment advisor, or insurance agent, determining whether to trust someone with your money really comes down to four things:

One: Do you feel the two of you would work well together?

When I say, "work well together," I mean, do you feel good about working with him as well as his staff?

Two: Is this a trustworthy person?

There are organizations that can help you gauge an advisor or company's trustworthiness.

For example, my company is a member of two such organizations: the Better Business Bureau and the National Ethics Association.

Before settling on a financial professional to work with, you can inquire to see if they are members of or rated by these organizations or similar ones.

Three: You need to feel that the person you work with knows what they are doing.

I've been in the business for more than twenty years. I've stayed in the game for a simple reason: I love what I do. Investing is an area in which I can help people, and "people helping people" is important to me.

I enjoy taking care of my clients. I always have. It drives me to continually learn all I can to help them.

I do regular reviews for my clients. Doing so is very important, but you know what? Some people basically take the money and run.

Some people are in this business one day, and the next they're not. People try real estate. They try mortgages. They try being a financial professional.

They're basically searching for a career that works for them: If they don't earn enough in this business, or it doesn't feel right, then they leave. They're more salespeople than advisors, searching for the right product to shill. When they move on to the next product, all the people they sold retirement accounts to have to find somebody else.

Many clients have told me a version of this story: "My son/friend/neighbor got into the business, so I got this product from him. Now he's not there anymore and I'm not sure what to do with it." There's a term we use for a client like this—an "orphan client." No different than leaving a stray 401(k).

You want to make sure that the person you're going to work with is going to stick around.

I'm proud that when people come into my office they see that we're in it for the long haul. We have an office, a staff, and a full team of dedicated professionals with a long history in the business.

Four: Your GUT! Your gut—what does it tell you?

———————

At the end of the day, whom you should work with is as simple as knowing who offers what and answering those four questions. The industry wants to make it seem complicated so that you feel that they're smarter than you. Its professionals want you to look at them in awe and say, "You can understand all this complicated stuff? I'm going to do business with you and not even question it."

But it isn't that complicated.

Chapter 3

MARKET MONEY,
FIVE-MINUTE MONEY, AND
PROTECTION WITH POWER MONEY

U   nderstanding the main investments, you can make,
         helps people make informed decisions. Many people
         get mixed up between their investments and the tax
status of their investments.

I remember asking a couple early in my career, "What type of investors are you?" The answer surprised me. They said, "We invest in IRAs." Interesting that they thought the *type* of investments they had was actually the *tax status* of their investments—which is important—but the type of investors they were is not the same thing. The **type of investor you are** relates to the type of investments you have made, such as stocks, bonds or mutual funds, annuities, and CDs, among other types of investments.

There are basically only three things that you can do with your money. I know the financial industry may not want you to recognize this, but in my opinion, it's as easy as the three things you can do with money when it comes to investing.

I feel you can categorize anything you can do with money as either the Market money, Five-Minute money, or Protection with Power money.

I'm dedicating an entire chapter to each type of money, but first, here are the basics of all three.

Market Money

What is Market money?

Market money refers to investments where your money is at risk of **losing money** and you **pay a fee** for the opportunity.

Defining characteristics

- **You** pay a fee.
- **You** take on risk.

Examples

- Stocks
- Bond funds (not to be confused with bonds; sometimes also called "fixed income")
- Corporate bonds
- Mutual funds
- ETFs (exchange-traded funds)
- REITs (real estate investment trusts)
- Variable annuities
- Gold
- Real estate

These are just some of many market investments. Market money includes *any* investment in which **you** pay a fee and take on **risk**. People sometimes ask me, "What about gold?"

I ask them, "Do you have to pay a fee?"

"Yes."

"Can you lose money?"

"Yes."

So, that would be a market investment.

"What about real estate?"

Same thing—you hire a realtor, so you pay a fee. Can you lose money? Well, we found out in 2008 that yes, you can.

Upside

- Your money has an opportunity to grow in the Market money.

Downside

- You must pay fees, and you can lose some or all of your money.

Five-Minute Money

What is Five-Minute money?

Five-Minute money is generally safer than Market money. However, at the time of this writing, Five-Minute money accounts typically don't have enough upside to keep up with inflation. Five-Minute money is important because you can easily draw from it in case of emergency. Everyone, I believe, should have Five-Minute money.

Defining characteristics

1. Relatively safe
2. Low upside
3. Usually (but not always) liquid

Examples

- Government bonds (**not** bond funds or corporate bonds—yes, they are different)
- Checking accounts
- Savings accounts
- CDs
- Money market accounts
- Fixed annuities not tied to an index

Upside
- Five-Minute money accounts are generally secure. Many Five-Minute money accounts are easy to withdraw money from when you need it.

Downside
- Five-Minute money accounts often do not earn enough to keep up with inflation. As a result, keeping too much money in the Five-Minute money account means that you are losing purchasing power over time.
- Some risk-averse investors look at the market and say, "I don't want to lose money, so I'll just keep all of my money [or too much] in a savings account." The problem is that technically they *are* losing money; their accounts don't keep up with inflation, so their money will be worth *less* as time goes on.
- Certain Five-Minute money accounts have annual fees or charges whenever your account dips below a certain balance. If you have a Five-Minute money account earning very low interest, these fees can eat up a significant portion of any returns, or even cut into your principal.

Protection with Power Money
Protection with Power money is secure **and** can grow with the market.

Defining characteristics

- Secure
- Potential growth with market upsides
- Partial liquidity
- Fixed-indexed annuities

Upside

- Your money is secure, *and* it can grow. I like to say you're getting the best of both worlds with the Protection with Power accounts, because you can keep up with inflation, and you can't lose your principal or your gains due to losses in the market.

- The Protection with Power accounts were never designed to grow faster than the market, and if the market is firing on all cylinders, it never would. However, with the volatility in the market over the past twenty years, sometimes Protection with Power accounts can perform better than market investments over time.

- Because Protection with Power accounts do not experience market losses, and they do participate in (reduced) gains when the market grows, they can jump into the lead when market investments lose value and need time to recover.

Downside

- Protection with Power accounts (fixed-indexed annuities) place limits on how much you can make. So, if the market spikes up, you won't earn *as much* in the Protection with Power accounts as you would in the market. That's the price you pay to protect your principal and your existing gains from market losses.

- There are many different Protection with Power accounts. Honestly, I don't like a lot of them because they don't meet my criteria for what I feel should and should not be in a Protection with Power–type of plan. For example, most of the time the plans that I offer don't have fees, but some others do have fees.

Warning: I have seen, and I have heard, some financial professionals will offer variable annuities with income riders and *suggest* that they are Protection with Power accounts (fixed-indexed annuities) or that they work the same way. Many companies put the terms "variable and fixed" on their statements, which can be confusing to consumers. Because of this, **many people with variable annuities understandably believe they have Protection with Power accounts (fixed-indexed annuities), which is not true. They have a variable annuity, which is Market money.**

Here's a rule that you can use to help spot this kind of misinformation: **A variable annuity is *not* a Protection**

with Power account (fixed-indexed annuity), and brokers cannot offer fixed-indexed annuities unless they hold a valid insurance license. However, brokers can offer *variable annuities*, which put your money in the market.

My personal investing philosophy: True diversification

I believe in true diversification across all three: Market money, Five-Minute money, and Protection with Power money. Having some at risk for the opportunity to grow, some secure and easy to withdraw, and some safe from market losses and growing enough to keep up with inflation.

What percentage of your money that you put each type of money will mostly come down to personal preferences and priorities, but there are a couple of rules of thumb that you can fall back on to guide you if you're not sure where to put your money.

The rule of one hundred

The rule of one hundred is a handy tool that can help you decide how much risk you should take with your investments.

The way it works is you subtract your age from one hundred. The number left over is the percentage of your money that you should have exposed to market fluctuations.

For example, if you applied the rule of one hundred at age seventy, you'd put 30 percent of your assets at risk in the market in one form or another.

True diversification means that among the 70 percent of your assets remaining, you hold investments in both the Five-Minute money (savings accounts, CDs, etc.) and the Protection with Power (fixed-indexed annuities).

The rule of four

The rule of four (also known as the **4 percent rule**) is a principle you can apply when withdrawing money. The concept is that if you withdraw 4 percent of your portfolio each year, then you *should never* run out of money.

To make the rule of four work, you must consider how safe your assets are, how much they will grow, how much money you need to survive, and how long you expect to draw money from that account.

Say you have $1,000,000 when you start taking money out—some of your assets in stocks, some in mutual funds, and some in bond funds. Per the rule of four, you would take out 4 percent a year ($40,000 in this case). In theory, you would never run out of money because your portfolio *should grow* by at least 4 percent each year.

However, this can be problematic if a lot of your assets are in the market and the market experiences a downward correction, as it did in 2000 and 2008.

At those times, the rule of four went out the window for many investors. If you pull 4 percent out, your financial professional grabs 2 percent, and the market takes out 30 percent, then you stand a good chance of running out of money.

Today, we can apply the rule of four to certain fixed-indexed annuities (unless you withdraw money from the annuity early), because you can avoid the risk of losing money in the market. In some cases, we can use a rule of *five* or even *six* for annual withdrawals and maintain a person's lifestyle and income for the rest of his or her life.

When considering withdrawal rates, it's important to remember that inflation will drive up your income needs. Thus, any income that you expect from investments must grow to keep up with the rise of your income needs. Think hard about income products that don't grow at least with inflation.

Where to put your money

The rules of one hundred and of four are good guidelines, but at the end of the day, it's your call. It is important to have true diversification across all three types of money. How you choose to allocate your investments across the three is ultimately up to you, depending on your goals and beliefs.

Some clients (usually younger investors) like to take more risk, so they may put more in the market. Others just want safety and liquidity, and they don't care as much about growth. So, they'll keep much or all their money in the Five-Minute money accounts.

Some people want it all—to keep their money secure *and* to have an opportunity to grow. They will likely gravitate toward the Protection with Power accounts, and they may not want to invest any money in the market.

To help you further understand the three types of money, we're going to dig deeper into each one, starting with Market money.

Chapter 4

MARKET MONEY

As we've discussed, investing in the market means that you pay a fee and take on risk. In this chapter, we'll go over the options you have for market investing in more detail, looking at their upsides and downsides.

If you're investing in the market, it's important to always keep your eyes open and see what you're investing in, because your money is at risk.

Many financial professionals often want you to ignore what's happening in the market, to "trust them," "have patience," "don't overreact to losses," and not to intervene.

Often, I've had clients tell me they called their financial professional and said, "I opened my statement today; I've lost a lot of money, and I can't sleep."

Rather than offering compassion or understanding, their financial professional's response was—you won't believe this—"Well, don't open your statement."

There are financial professionals that have really said that: *Don't open your statement.*

Try that with the electric company and see what happens.

No matter what you've heard before, **you should open your statement**. You should know where your money is, and how it's doing. At the end of the day, it's your money. So, here's what you can do with it in market:

Market investing options

Stocks

Buying a stock is simple. Buying the right stock can be a challenge. When you buy a stock, you're purchasing a piece of ownership (a share) in a publicly traded company.

Stocks allow you to participate in a company's profits and losses through capital gains/losses and through dividends (money paid out to shareholders from profits).

Stocks can return the best yields in the market because they are often the riskiest. If the company you invest in has problems, then the stock price may tumble, eroding your investment. The company could also go bankrupt, in which case you may lose all the money that you invested in that stock.

You must pay fees when you buy and sell stocks, and the cost varies based on whom you buy from. Full-service investment firms may charge commissions or percentage-based annual fees on a stock portfolio, while discount brokers may charge a small fee on each trade (usually between $5 and $30 per transaction).

Typically, people buy stocks and hold them for a set period. You can sell a stock right away if you want; you don't have to wait for the day's closing bell, as you do with certain other investments.

Some people have picked some good stocks and have done well. Other people buy the stock of the company that employs them because they want to own part of the company they work for.

Keep the following in mind when investing in stocks: Every time you sell a stock, somebody else is buying.

Only one of you can be right.

Beware of jumping on a stock that you hear is a winner. There's a term for this: "If it's in the paper, it's in the price." If you see a report on a rising stock in the newspaper or on the internet, the growth may have *already happened*, and the price has jumped up accordingly.

Hop on board at that point and you very well may find yourself overpaying for a stock or fund that has peaked and perhaps is on its way down or may only have minor growth left.

Bond Funds

A bond fund (otherwise known as a "fixed income" or "bond mutual fund") is **very different** from a traditional bond. A traditional bond may go up or down in value, but if you hold it until maturity, then in most cases you will receive no less than your original investment.

On the other hand, when you purchase a bond fund (fixed-income fund), you pay a manager a fee and they invest your money into an array of corporate bonds, junk bonds, municipalities, government bonds, and similar products that go up and down in value. There is no maturity date and no guarantee that you will receive your initial investment back.

Here are four key differences between bond funds and traditional bonds:

1. **No guaranteed return of original investment:** Bond funds have no obligation to return your principal.

Even if the words "fixed income" or "bond" are in the name, that doesn't mean your principal is safe.

2. **Fluctuating interest:** The interest you receive on a bond fund can fluctuate with changes to the bond portfolio. Many bond funds pay interest monthly, while most traditional bonds pay interest semiannually.

3. **Liquidity:** Virtually all bond funds can be sold easily at any time at their current value. On the other hand, the liquidity of individual bonds varies quite a bit. In addition to taking longer to sell, traditional bonds may be more expensive to sell.

4. **Diversification:** A bond fund may provide instant diversification. However, it's important to understand that you are buying a bond fund, *which can lose value*, and not a traditional bond.

The upside of bond funds often isn't as high as other market options, and generally the downside isn't as bad either.

However, the problem with bond funds, as we found out in 2008, is that they still can lose money—**some bond funds lost 10 percent to 40 percent during the recession.**[7]

We have been conditioned to feel that if a broker sells us a corporate bond, then it is safe: "This is a great company. Nothing will ever happen to it."

---

7   Hale, "Oppenheimer's Bond-Fund Blowup: Worse Than You Think."

I've heard this about too many "great companies" before. **Blockbuster. Circuit City. Enron.** If you bought corporate bonds in these companies, where did your money go when they went bankrupt?

Mutual Funds

A mutual fund refers to a group of investors putting money into a fund that an investment company (manager) oversees. The manager invests the fund into groups of stocks and bond funds and sells shares of the fund that you can buy through a broker.

The value of the mutual fund changes as the performance of the various stocks and bond funds within it go up or down. Mutual funds provide more diversity than individual stocks.

Mutual funds have several challenges:

- The fees are high.
- There are limitations on trading them.
- You are the only one taking on risk—the broker makes money regardless of whether you earn money or lose it.
- There are lower-fee alternatives, such as ETFs.

High fees

Compared to other investment options, mutual funds can be expensive as far as fees are concerned. You pay fees constantly, some of which you don't even see. Here are some of the fees you pay in a mutual fund:

1. Load fees
2. Transaction fees
3. Fund expenses
4. Management fees
5. Administrative costs (like postage, record keeping, and more)
6. Marketing and sales costs (called the "12b-1 fee")

You may also pay:

- Purchase fees when you buy a fund
- Exchange fees if you choose to transfer into a different fund
- Redemption fees when you sell

Brokers often quote you at 1 percent for **their fee**, but their fee is only **one of many fees that you're paying.** When including all the fees, a mutual fund **may cost up to 4 percent.**

Meanwhile, most people think they're paying 1 percent because the other fees come right out of the fund before they receive their earnings statements. There is a lot of industry jargon to wade through to even *find* the fees that you are paying.

If you pay a financial professional for a mutual fund, he's selling you a mutual fund that already has a money manager, who also gets paid. The money manager takes her fee right out of the fund, so you may not ever know what the fee is. You would have to read the prospectus for that fund—fifty-some pages and the fees are mixed in.

If the fund grew 3 percent in the market, you may see only a 1 percent or 2 percent return on your statement; the report that you receive on the fund's performance only states the performance of your investment **after the fund manager has taken his percent or portion.**

The same rule applies when the fund goes down. If the fund goes down 10 percent and the fund manager's fee is 1.5 percent, in most cases you'll simply receive an 11.5 percent loss on your statement, without seeing the breakdown between market losses and management fees.

Fees take away your market upside, **but you're taking on more than 100 percent of the risk:** When the market goes down, you lose your money, *and* you must pay the fee *on top of* the market loss.

Some financial professionals will often justify their fees by saying, "Yes, the fund is expensive, but it's *so good*."

They condition people to believe that the more they pay, the better the fund. I met with someone recently (who is now a new client of mine), and that's what his financial professional told him repeatedly. He was conditioned through years of sales pitches to believe that higher fees equal better funds.

He had a $100,000 investment in a few "good mutual funds"—and he lost $3,000 in two and a half years.

Here's the kicker—he had to pay another **$4,000 in fees for the privilege of that $3,000 loss.**

Is that just an isolated incident? Do the most expensive funds usually perform better than cheaper ones?

Not according to Warren Buffett, who said that index funds in the market (such as the S&P 500) will generally outperform expensive, managed funds.[8] If you check *Forbes*, you will also see that *"higher-expense funds do not, on average, perform better than lower-expense funds."*[9]

So, they can't tell me that one must pay more for a better fund.

The idea that managed funds are better than lower-expense funds comes from marketing—mutual fund managers need to promote their funds to justify their fees. They often engage in processes to make their funds look better, such as "window dressing."

Window dressing refers to a practice by which fund managers buy high-performing stocks *after the growth has happened* near the end of the quarter, before issuing a report to shareholders. They do this to tout that they bought a high-

---

8   Reuters, "Warren Buffett Bashes Hedge Funds at Annual Meeting," *Fortune*, May 1, 2016, http://fortune.com/2016/04/30/warren-buffett-hedge-funds/.

9   Simon Moore, "Get More by Paying Less for Your Funds," *Forbes*, September 29, 2014, http://www.forbes.com/sites/simonmoore/2014/09/29/get-more-by-paying-less-for-your-funds/#3679e1476320.

performing stock—even though they didn't have it when it performed well.

High fees represent the biggest catch to mutual funds: Many often have too many hands in the cookie jar for the client to benefit properly.

Trading limitations

Also, you can't sell mutual funds at a moment's notice the way you can with stocks or exchange-traded funds (ETFs).

This is important.

Say you have a mutual fund, and you notice the market correcting down at 10:00 a.m.; you want to sell. You could put in an order to sell the fund at 10:00 a.m., but you will only be able to sell it for the closing price that day, when trading ends at 4:00 p.m.

In the meantime, you will be forced to watch helplessly all day as that fund could drop by any amount before 4:00 p.m., while you can do nothing to get out and preserve your money.

Lower fee alternatives: ETFs

The biggest question for me personally is: Why buy mutual funds when you could have an ETF portfolio? ETFs have lower fees, they can be more diversified, they have fewer restrictions, and they often perform better.

Mutual funds are just so expensive, and the fees eat up your money in my opinion. Why are you paying those fees?

What are the fund managers trying to do? They're trying to match an index, such as the S&P 500.

Why pay to *try* to match an index when you can just buy an ETF that *directly* tracks the index—without the high fees?

ETFs (Exchange-Traded Funds)

ETFs are groups of diverse assets that trade on an exchange like stocks. Many market investors find ETFs attractive because of their diversification, tax efficiency, liquidity, performance, and low fees.

Diversification is very important in the market. If you're going to have your money at risk, you should be as diversified as possible. ETFs can often provide more diversification than other market options, including mutual funds.

Say you own ten mutual funds, and each mutual fund owns stock in ten companies; then your money is diversified into one hundred companies.

That may seem like a lot, but if you have an ETF portfolio tracking a few different indexes, your investment can be spread across many more companies.

Say you invest some money in an ETF that tracks the S&P 500—that's 500 companies. Then you do the same with the Russell 2000—that's 2,000 companies. If you also invest in an ETF tracking the Nasdaq 100, that's another hundred companies. With just those three ETFs, your money is already spread across 2,600 companies. That's far more diversification than mutual funds or individual stocks will get you.

You can use ETFs to diversify across industry or country lines too. There are hundreds of ETFs available; they cover every major index (issued by Dow Jones, S&P, and Nasdaq) and sector of the equities market. There are international, regional (Europe, Pacific Rim, emerging markets), and country-specific (Japan, Australia, UK) ETFs. Specialized ETFs even cover specific industries (technology, biotech, energy) and market niches (REITs, gold).

ETFs also cover other asset classes, such as fixed income, including ETFs composed of long-term bonds, mid-term bonds, and short-term bonds.

On top of the diversity they can provide, ETFs can be very tax-efficient—you can often defer taxes on your ETF portfolio until you sell.

ETFs are liquid investments as well; unlike mutual funds, ETFs can be sold at any point in the trading day.

Perhaps the biggest advantage of ETFs is their low annual fees relative to most mutual funds. Purchasing ETFs is like buying stocks; whenever you buy and sell an ETF you pay a brokerage fee, usually ranging from a few dollars per trade up to $20 per trade. These purchase fees can make it cost-prohibitive to invest a little bit at a time into ETFs.

However, for lump-sum investors, the brokerage fees are often insignificant compared to the savings that come from the ETF's low annual fees. While a mutual fund might cost anywhere from 1 percent to 4 percent in annual fees,[10] ETFs are virtually free; they usually cost about 0.5 percent in annual expenses.[11]

The value of low annual fees is enormous.

Vanguard (one of the largest investment firms in the world), investigated the impact of annual fees on investments. They compared two investments, each with a starting value of $100,000. In one fund, the investor paid 0.25 percent in fees each year, and in the other, the investor paid 0.90 percent.

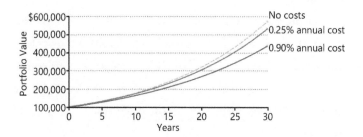

This chart is for illustrative purposes and is not intended to be representative of any specific investment vehicle. Past performance is not indicative of future results.

10 Brett Carson, "The Mutual Fund Fees We Don't Talk About," *U.S. News*, March 4, 2015, http://money.usnews.com/money/blogs/the-smarter-mutual-fund-investor/2015/03/04/the-mutual-fund-fees-we-dont-talk-about.

11 "How to Choose an Exchange-Traded Fund (ETF)," *Wall Street Journal*, accessed February 23, 2017, http://guides.wsj.com/personal-finance/investing/how-to-choose-an-exchange-traded-fund-etf/.

Vanguard set both investments' growth at 6 percent annually over thirty years. They found that the difference between 0.25 percent and 0.90 percent in annual fees amounted **to a difference of nearly $100,000** in accumulated value over those thirty years.[12]

How does that "1 percent" that your broker charges look now?

As you can see, even with consistent, strong growth in your investment, fees can eat up an enormous amount of your money.

On the other hand, if you invest in an ETF tracking the S&P 500, it's virtually free, from a fees perspective. Lower fees do not mean worse returns. From a performance standpoint, ETFs are very competitive. Warren Buffett has stated that the S&P 500 will outperform most professional investment managers.[13]

Younger investors primarily looking for growth in the market thus may consider buying ETFs early and holding them for the long haul.

Once you're closing in on retirement, you have less time on your side, so the "set it and forget it" model is not as practical. At that stage, we could consider adjusting your ETF portfolio to diversify it and protect your money a little more, or to take it out of the market entirely. As you get older,

---

12 Vanguard, *Vanguard's Principles for Investing Success* (2014), http://www.vanguard.com/pdf/s700.pdf.

13 Reuters, "Warren Buffett Bashes Hedge Funds at Annual Meeting."

I usually say that it's better to keep money safer (out of the market), because whenever you're in the market, even in an ETF, there is risk.

Real Estate

As we went over in chapter 3, real estate is in the Market money—you must pay a fee to purchase it, and your money is at risk. Real estate investing is far more hands-on than some other Market money options. To succeed in real estate, you the investor will usually need some specialized knowledge on the subject.

I am not an expert in real estate investing, and I don't pretend to be, either. If you're considering real estate, you should do more research on the subject. Keep in mind that true diversification means also having some money in the Five-Minute money and Protection with Power accounts. So even if you do plan on investing in real estate, remember that it is only *part of* a balanced portfolio.

Gold/Other Commodities

Investing in commodities means investing in goods such as gold, metals, grains, oils, livestock, and other tangible items. People ask me about gold and silver all the time. I usually tell them it's OK if it meets their goals and risk tolerance—after all, those investments can easily lose money.

You could diversify your risky investments to limit your risk in any one sector by owning a variety of market products: Stocks, ETFs, bond funds, and commodities.

Variable Annuities

Variable annuities are insurance products. They're a bit complicated, but in short, you invest some money and pay a fee for features like income riders (a guaranteed income stream). The annuity gives you an income stream based on the performance of the funds you choose or the riders that you pay to add. Variable annuities may also have a death benefit rider option.

Variable annuities are often marketed as safe—but they're not. You can lose your prior earnings and principal. Variable annuities are not FDIC-insured, and while they may be marketed with words like "guaranteed," if you read the fine print, these funds come with a long and boring prospectus explaining how they work.

They are often marketed as having a 5 percent to 7 percent interest rate guaranteed, but that's misleading as well. Chapter 8 of this book explains how these claims are misleading, exposes the facts of variable annuities, and clears the air behind the smoke and mirrors used to sell them.

Variable annuities are expensive. The *Wall Street Journal* says that variable annuity fees can reach about 4 percent per year. As we've gone over, fees erode your growth—**the 4 percent in fees can limit your returns by about 50 percent**.[14]

Here are some of the fees you'll pay with a variable annuity:

---

14 "Are Variable Annuities a Good Investment?" *Wall Street Journal*, May 14, 2012, https://www.wsj.com/articles/SB1000142405270230 3916904577376193314287640.

- M&E (management and expenses)
- Administration
- GMIB (guaranteed minimum income benefit)
- GMDB (guaranteed minimum death benefit)
- Cost of the actual funds within the annuity

Variable annuities may often be marketed in a misleading fashion, and almost always come with an income rider, which usually means even more fees. I've devoted all of chapter 8 in this book to explaining how income riders really work, including the pros and cons, but here's a brief overview:

An income rider guarantees you income every month—but you pay a fee for it, and you start by taking your own money out. It often takes quite a while (think decades, not years) to get any new money; the income does not go up with inflation. And when all is said and done, you don't receive nearly as high of a return as marketers often advertise. I believe ANY income option needs to have an increasing option. Although a case could be made for someone older or sickly to receive as much up front as possible. It is so important in my opinion to work with a person who can look at your personal situation and make recommendations based on *your* needs, not theirs.

REITs (Real Estate Investment Trusts)

REITs are trusts that invest in real estate, either in properties that the trust owns or in mortgages that they purchase.

You can buy shares in REITs the same way that you would in a mutual fund. REITs pay dividends to their investors, making them attractive to some investors looking for income. However, like all market investments, REITs come with the risk of losing some or all of your money, and no return is guaranteed.

There are two types of REITs—traded and non-traded. Simply put, this refers to whether they can be traded on the open market.

Be cautious with REITs, especially non-traded ones, because they can be hard to sell. I find that many people with REITs have non-traded.

REITS may offer a nice return on investment, but there's a difference between getting a **return on** your money and getting the **return of** your money. To get out of a REIT, you must find a buyer or the REIT managers need to do a repurchase offer. This makes them hard to liquidate.

Non-traded REITs invest in real estate with the intent of turning a profit by selling the real estate to another investor or later offering the REIT to the public. The cycle for the investment is usually seven to ten years.

I've seen so many clients who want to get out of a REIT yet need to wait it out until there's a repurchase offer. While they wait, their money is tied up and they can't get at it.

Some will argue that you can get a return of around 8 percent. That's great, but if you're going to have a challenge getting your money back, what good is the growth?

What's the upside of market investing?

When the market is doing fantastically well, of course you want to be in it. The upside in the market is higher than in the other two types of money.

You may want to balance across all types of money even when the market is booming, because nobody has a crystal ball to know how long the growth will last, and there is always risk in the market.

If you are looking to invest in the market, be sure to consider the fees, liquidity, and diversification offered by each investment option, so you can make the best possible decision for your needs.

The upside of winning usually doesn't outweigh the pain of losing

They tell almost everyone, be in the market and watch your life savings go up and down, repeatedly. I think you need to be careful. The upside isn't as important to me as safety because the benefit of winning doesn't usually outweigh the pain of losing.

Look at it this way: Say you're coming up on retirement, or you're already retired. If you took your entire savings and doubled it, how would your life change?

You might go out to eat a little bit more, take a few more vacations, help the kids out a little more. But most of the time you're going to hang out with the same friends, stay in the same house, and go to the same restaurants.

But let's look at it the other way: What if Wall Street comes crashing down, and you **lose half of your money.** Is your lifestyle going to change?

Absolutely.

You could lose your house, or not be able to go out to eat. Look at any time in history when the market had a correction. Retirement is the time to reap the rewards of your sacrifices and hard work. It is not the time you should be trying to recapture money that you used to own.

Market risk can take all of that away: If you retire at sixty-five, just as the market crashes, you might have to wait until you're seventy-five to get the money back that you lost. At that point, who knows? Your health might not be good.

You've also lost ten years that you should have been enjoying. Those years are never coming back, even if the market recovers.

The market can take it away more quickly than it gives it back

The problem with the market when you're close to retirement is that losses often happen much quicker than gains, making it easy to lose a lot of money and hard to gain it back.

At my seminars, I ask the audience: "Say the market goes down 20 percent this year, but next year, it goes right back up 20 percent. You're back where you were, right?"

A lot of people say yes.

While it seems logical, that's incorrect.

When you lose 20 percent, you need to earn 25 percent to break even.

If you lose 25 percent, then you need to earn 33 percent to break even. Or, if you experience the 40 percent losses that many did in 2000 and 2008, **you need to earn 67 percent to break even.**

The math may seem tricky, but the reason behind it is that when the market loses *and then* recovers, you're **recovering from a position of less money.**

If you start with $100,000, a 20 percent loss is $20,000. That leaves you with $80,000. To make $20,000 *from a position of $80,000*, the market must go up by 25 percent, because $20,000 is 25 percent of $80,000, **which is all you have left.** The $20,000 you already lost isn't there to help you grow. Remember, neither are the fees that have been taken directly out of your account.

The market can drop by 20 percent in a flash, but it may take years to go up 25 percent—and at that point, you've only *broken even,* **not accounting for the fees** you're paying the entire time it takes to recover.

With the market, you're gambling on timing. If you're in the market at the right time, you can make money. But if you're not, and the market drops at the same time you need to start withdrawing money, you can be in big trouble, and the market likely won't recover fast enough to save even your principal. You'll lose too much of what you had.

Let's take the same $100,000 example and say you're drawing 5 percent a year for income ($5,000). Now, if the market **crashes** and your portfolio go down to say, $50,000, you still need your $5,000, but now to get it, you're taking 10 percent out.

So, you take out the $5,000 you need, and you're down to $45,000. Even if everything in your portfolio starts to go up, *it's going up from the position of $45,000*—the growth means less actual money than it did for your original portfolio.

Even in the unlikely event that the market shoots right back up 50 percent—the same amount that it just dropped— then you **are still down to $67,500.** You've lost around $30,000, and you'll still need to draw more money for income, making it even harder to regain your principal.

The longer you must pull from a reduced portfolio, the more the losses compound, and the harder it is *to make your own money back,* let alone to see it grow. But you still need money, whether the market is up or down.

Some financial professionals don't want you to recognize that when the market has corrections, it can correct anywhere from 20 percent to 60 percent. When they talk about corrections, they'll say, "Maybe we're in for a correction of 10 percent." It's hard to even hear them say 20 percent. But bigger losses happen, and if they happen at the wrong time, you can be in big trouble.

Losses at the wrong time can mean that you run out of money

I enjoy helping clients considering income options, because I have many clients who need to pull money from their investments. That's why it kills me when a financial professional acts like a 5 percent loss is nothing, telling someone, "Don't worry about it, it'll come right back up."

If you're using a system like the rule of four to pull income out of your investments, then **a 5 percent loss means you lost a full year's worth of income!**

However, *you didn't lose a full year of expenses*. The market dropping 5 percent doesn't mean that your bills magically disappeared. So, if you're relying on your investment accounts for income, you'll still have to pull out money while the market is down, further endangering your principal.

For many years, people drew money from their accounts following the rule of four. However, when the market came crashing down in 2000 and again in 2008, that strategy had challenges to say the least. Today, according to several experts, a successful use of the rule of four may be an *exception* and not the rule.[15]

When you examine the disastrous effect of market losses at a time when you need to withdraw money, it's easy to see why the rule of four may no longer work for many investors.

---

15 Jon Stein, "The 4% Retirement Rule Is Broken," *CNBC*, November 4, 2014, http://www.cnbc.com/2014/11/03/the-4-retirement-rule-is-broken-and-heres-why.html.

Let's use a $100,000 account as an example, and say you withdraw 4 percent each year—that's $4,000. The market crashes, and now the account is worth $60,000. Regardless of the market, you still need that $4,000. However, you're now taking $4,000 from $60,000, which is 6.5 percent, so the whole "rule of four" falls apart.

In that scenario, for you to be able to pull the income that you need, your money would have to grow at an average of 6.5 percent each year going forward to keep up. If your money does not grow that fast, then you're likely to run out.

These aren't simply hypothetical situations. According to the investment firm T. Rowe Price, if you retired January 1, 2000, and applied the rule of four (accounting for withdrawal increases to meet inflation) to a portfolio based on roughly equal portions of stocks and bonds, you'd most likely run out of money within fewer than thirty years.[16]

Studies show that the number one thing retirees are afraid of isn't death. It's running out of money. You know how people run out of money? You've heard it ever since you were a kid: "Too many hands in the cookie jar."

In many market accounts, there are often too many hands in the cookie jar. You put your investment money in the "jar," and your financial professional comes in to take money out (his fees); you take some money out for income, whether it's 4 percent, 5 percent, or 6 percent. Then, suddenly, the market

---

16   Kelly Greene, "Say Goodbye to the 4% Rule," *Wall Street Journal*, March 3, 2013, https://www.wsj.com/articles/SB1000142412788732416230457830449149255984.

has a correction. Depending on the losses, the market puts two or three hands in the cookie jar for its 20 percent or 30 percent.

How long do you think your money will last? If people keep taking and taking and taking, at a certain point, there won't be anything left.

There have been strong times in the stock market, but during the past twenty years it has been very volatile, and that's dangerous for people coming up on retirement. Should you count on the market adding enough into your cookie jar, more than what you and the broker take out?

When is a good time to invest in the market?

There are different stages of life. **Between the ages of twenty and fifty is a growth stage.** During that time, I believe, you should be all about growth, which may involve market investments.

Why? The growth opportunity is there, and you have time on your side to recover from market corrections.

Sometimes my clients will ask me to meet with their children who are in their twenties or thirties. When I meet with younger people, I give them the same advice that I give my son. I think it's good advice because I learned it from listening to Warren Buffett.

"You know what, son? When you're putting money into your retirement account, just buy an ETF that tracks the S&P 500. There are virtually no fees, and over thirty, forty years, you're probably going to be better off than if you're paying broker fees in a mutual fund." Ouch, I bet brokers don't like hearing this.

For someone around thirty years old, it's all about growth; that person is not going to retire for thirty to forty years. Buying an index fund gives him or her that opportunity, and safety is not as high of a priority at first.

I can't give that same advice to somebody fifty. **Fifty is the magic number** for most people, when you move into the **preservation stage** and begin to get serious about protecting your money for retirement.

If you keep most of your money in the market and the market has a significant drop, it might take ten years just to get back to where you were. If you're fifty or sixty years old, you can't afford to wait for the whims of an unpredictable market; you need that money to grow or at the very least to **stay stable**.

Many of my clients are coming up on retirement or already retired, and I help them preserve capital and earn a reasonable return to keep up with inflation and taxes.

In our **seventies,** we tend to move into the **distribution stage.** We should continue to keep our money safe from market losses *and* earn a reasonable rate of return so that we don't run out of money as we start to withdraw from our nest egg.

How much should you put in the market?

As far as how much to put in the market, it really comes down to your own risk tolerance. You can turn to the rule of one hundred as a guide, but it's most important to realize that you can lose some or all of the money you have in the market.

You should only risk what you are prepared to lose. If you can't afford to lose money, then why put money in the market? Told you it would be simple.

Chapter 5

FIVE-MINUTE MONEY

T he Five-minute money refers to secure money that may not grow fast enough to keep up with inflation.

Upside

- Secure
- Liquid

Downside

- Money typically won't grow fast enough to keep up with inflation.

- Accounts with fees can limit returns and, in some cases, damage principal.

Types of Five-Minute money accounts

- Traditional bank accounts such as:
  - ○ Checking accounts
  - ○ Savings accounts
  - ○ Money market accounts
- Certificates of deposit (CDs)
- Traditional bonds
- Fixed annuities *not tied to an index* (These are **not to be confused with fixed-indexed annuities** [see chapter 6, *Protection with Power*]. A fixed annuity that is not tied to an index is an insurance product that works very similarly to a bond or a CD—you put away your money for a period and earn a set interest rate. The problem with fixed annuities is that interest rates are currently not high enough to keep up with inflation.)

Five-Minute money is meant to be where you save money before you "invest" anything. You may want to keep six to nine months' worth of living expenses in Five-Minute money, just in case of emergency.

Of course, everybody asks, "Is there any way that I can keep my money liquid, safe, and get a 5 percent or higher return?"

Today, the answer is no.

Five-Minute money accounts such as checking, savings, and money market accounts are all liquid, but you'd be lucky to earn 2 percent interest. If you want to earn a little more on your money in the Five-Minute money, then you must opt for something like a bank CD—but then you're giving up liquidity for a little more interest.

What to look for in the Five-Minute money

- Liquidity—easy access to your money
- A bank that you like
- Fee-free accounts

Really, there is not a ton of difference among Five-Minute money accounts. Find a bank that you like, an account that makes it easy to access your funds and doesn't charge too many fees, and you're good to go.

Current interest rates have me calling bank CDs "certificates of disappointment." Right now, the interest that you can earn on a bank CD is so minimal that it may not be worth restricting access to your money.

Back in the day when the ten-year treasury notes or bonds paid 4 percent or 5 percent, they were a good counterbalance to risky stocks. Those bonds don't pay that well anymore, so the balancing act doesn't work.

Today, it's like you've got a 400-pound person (your risky Market money investments) on one side of a seesaw, and a 90-pound person (your safer savings or CDs) on the other side. The 90-pound featherweight doesn't offer much resistance when the 400-pound heavyweight starts hurtling toward the earth.

When should you consider investing in the Five-Minute money?

The Five-Minute money can be very helpful for protecting your other investments. I like to use the Five-Minute money, or emergency money to have available if you lose your job, if your kids need money, or if your refrigerator breaks and you need to buy a new one.

Here's how the Five-Minute money can help you protect your investments: Say you have an emergency and you need cash. If you only have money in the market and the market is down, you're hurting your assets by taking money out—plus, depending on how you're invested, you may have to pay penalties to take it out.

The Five-Minute money is an important part of the equation as an emergency fund and to help with unexpected expenses. However, it is not an investment tool because although it is secure you most likely won't earn enough interest to keep up with inflation.

How much should you keep in Five-Minute money accounts?

A good rule of thumb is to keep six to nine months' worth of living expenses in the Five-Minute money accounts.

There is a downside to keeping too much money in the Five-Minute money accounts. You miss the opportunity for your money to grow or even to keep up with inflation. Trillions of dollars in the United States are sitting in Five-Minute money accounts right now and not making their owners any money.

So how much is too much?

Let's say nine months of your living expenses equals $45,000, but you have $200,000 sitting in the Five-Minute money accounts—that would probably be too much. You could potentially move $100,000 to earn some more interest without giving up much security, and you'd still have plenty of liquid cash in case of an emergency.

Caveat: You **can lose money** in certain Five-Minute money accounts if they have **deferral periods** and you take your money out early. For example, if you agree to put your money in a CD for five years and you take it out after only three years, you may have to pay a penalty, so you may lose money.

Chapter 6

PROTECTION WITH POWER

You will not believe this, but there is a way in which a person can have Protection with Power. Protection with Power products have two defining characteristics: They are **safe from market losses**, and they have the potential for **market upside.**

The general idea of a Protection with Power product is that when the market goes up, you can earn new money, but you don't lose any money when the market goes down.

The proper term for these accounts is "fixed-indexed annuities." What I call them is Protection with Power products.

Benefits of Protection with Power products (fixed-indexed annuities)

- Your money is safe from market losses.
- You can grow with the market.
- Your money can grow tax-deferred, so you don't pay taxes on your gains until you withdraw your money.
- There are no purchase fees.
- There are no management fees—100 percent of your money goes to work for you unless you buy an income rider.

Even though I'm licensed to offer just about every type of investment available, I specialize in the Protection with Power accounts because I believe that it is often a great place for those coming up on retirement or retired to invest some of their money. I consider myself a safe-money guy, and the Protection with Power accounts offer the best of both worlds—security and the opportunity for growth.

The philosophy behind prioritizing safety in your investments goes back more than a century. The great Mark

Twain is often credited with first saying, "It's not the return *on* my money that I'm interested in, it's the return *of* my money."

With a Protection with Power account, your money is protected from market losses because it never actually goes into the market. It's not a security like a stock or mutual fund—it's an insurance product.

However, you *can* participate in the market's upside by linking the annuity to one or more indexes, such as the S&P 500, the Nasdaq 100, or the Russell 2000.

Because fixed-indexed annuities are not securities, some feel they are generally simpler than market products.

If you buy a mutual fund, you'll receive a fifty-some page prospectus with it to explain what you just bought—a good booklet if you have insomnia. Within about two pages you'll be asleep. They're long, hard to understand, and boring.

Protection with Power accounts don't have a prospectus; they have what's called a "statement of understanding," or some sort of discloser pages outlining the benefits and limitations in their product. It is usually 4 to 18 pages. I feel, and have been told, it is so much easier to understand.

The Protection with Power accounts work more like bonds used to when they were paying 4 percent to 5 percent—you invest money up front, you wait a certain amount of time (usually between five and ten years), and then you collect your money with earnings. You typically have an option to withdraw 10 percent a year without penalty in case you need income or a withdrawal.

Most annuities are sold in lump sums. However, there are some "flexible premiums" annuities in which the provider will allow you to contribute more money after the initial purchase (usually within the first year).

They operate Protection with Power accounts from the *yield of their portfolios* (their profits), so it's no real risk to their core assets.

Insurance companies follow the adage, "Slow and steady wins the race." They generally have less overhead than other large companies. Think about the providers of other investment options, like broker houses and banks— they have branches all over the place. Insurance companies will usually have one main office in the country, which is much more cost-effective. Think about this. How many drug stores are on just about every corner. Do you feel prescriptions are higher than they should be? Perhaps some of the costs of running so many stores play a role in the high costs associated with prescription medicines (just saying). There increasingly are drug stores opening on corners across the United States. I pulled up to a street corner years back and saw a drive-through. I was hungry, so I pulled in. I ordered a burger, fries, and a soda. The lady over the intercom said, "We are a pharmacy, do you need a prescription filled?"

"No," I said, "I am just hungry."

She said, "We have a pill for that."

Many different Protection with Power account features

There is a ton of variety among Protection with Power accounts. Knowing what to look for and what to avoid is key, you can find attractive plans with a lot of benefits.

Unfortunately, there is a ton of misinformation online about annuities, making it difficult to evaluate them properly.

Why is there so much misinformation? Well, in recent years a lot of investors have moved money from the market to the Protection with Power accounts. As a result, some people who make their money by offering market investments write hit pieces about competing options to try to lure people back to their products. These "experts" seize on the downsides of **some** annuities as evidence to claim that "*all* annuities are bad."

Because of this, a Google search for "annuities" will often lead to blogs and articles bashing **all** annuities, blanketing an entire balance of money as negative based on the catches of a few products—many times, mixing variable and fixed-indexed annuities together. This is misleading and not accurate. Variable annuities and fixed-indexed annuities are as different as oranges and apples. If someone doesn't know that, be wary.

As we all know, just because something is on the internet doesn't mean it is true. There are good annuities and bad annuities, but the negative features of the bad ones don't affect the good annuities that don't have those catches.

With all the noise online, it can be hard to find accurate, unbiased information on annuities or other investments. As a result, many people struggle to find out which annuities are good for them and which are not right for their needs.

Our clients' financial well-being is too important for us to rely on the common knowledge available to the public via Google and other outlets, which can be manipulated by marketers and misinformation.

To find accurate information and give quality advice to clients, my team and I devote extensive research resources to evaluating investment options, including exclusive software and detailed annuity information that comes directly from providers.

We devote time and care to studying the details of each one of the hundreds of annuities on the market to discover their upsides and their downsides so that we can find the best ones to meet our clients' individual needs.

Fixed-indexed annuities vs. variable annuities: Worlds of difference

Protection with Power (fixed-indexed annuities) and variable annuities (market) may sound similar—for starters, they both have the word "annuity" in them—but they are actually very different. **Variable annuities are in the market (you**

can lose money), and fixed-indexed annuities are secure (not in the market).

Variable annuities often come with riders and additional fees. For example, it's been years since I've seen a variable annuity sold without an income rider.

Some financial professionals, and certainly not all, sell clients on variable annuities by telling them, "Listen, no matter what happens, we're going to guarantee that you'll receive 5 percent, 6 percent, or 7 percent." Clients then think that they can't lose money in the variable annuity, but that's not true—the "guaranteed return" is a smoke and mirrors sales tactic, if offered that way. (see chapter 8 for more on this).

Most of the time when clients come in to see me and they have a variable annuity with an income rider they'll tell me, "I have the Protection with Power account," or "I can't lose any of my cash value."

This is false.

It's very important to learn the distinction between fixed-indexed annuities and variable annuities: Fixed indexed equals *safe from market losses*. Variable equals *risk and fees*.

However, people are starting to notice it. Variable annuities have gone down in popularity, and demand for Protection with Power (fixed-indexed annuities) has increased.

When should you consider investing in the Protection with Power accounts? When you are starting to think about retirement or looking to protect your principal or some part of it, while still benefitting from potential market gains.

Chapter 7

QUALIFIED MONEY VS. NONQUALIFIED MONEY, AND WHY IT MATTERS

Whether money is "qualified" or not refers to how the investment is taxed. There are two types of tax statuses: qualified and not qualified. The difference between the two is simple: Do you pay taxes now or do you pay taxes later?

For qualified money, you pay taxes at the time you withdraw your money. Nonqualified money is taxed in the year you earn it.

Qualified money

Another term for qualified money is "tax-deferred" money. Qualified money means that you deduct the amount that you invest from your income tax returns for the year in which you invest; that is, you **do not** pay taxes on it at the time you invest. Instead, when you take the money out, you are taxed on the principal and the interest.

Companies often set up qualified plans for employees that allow them to invest money from their paychecks and lower their taxable income.

Here's how qualified money works in the real world: Let's say you made $1,000 a week and you tucked away $100 of that into a qualified account. From a tax perspective that year, it's as if you earned $900 a week.

You pay taxes that year on the $900. The other $100 goes into your retirement investment account. Then, whenever you take the money out, you pay taxes on the entire value, including interest, as if it is ordinary income during the withdrawal year.

Examples of qualified money

- 401(k) or 403(b) plans offered by your employer (For many people, these are the easiest and best ways to start investing for retirement.)

- SEP IRA (simplified employee pension IRA; for the self-employed)

- SIMPLE IRA (savings investment match plan for employees IRA; for the self-employed)
- Traditional IRA
- Roth IRA (This one is really in its own category— more on it in a bit.)
- Health Savings Account (HSA)
- TSA (tax-sheltered annuity)
- 457 plans (These are plans for government employees. They have attributes of both qualified and nonqualified investments.)

Early withdrawals and required minimum distributions (RMDs)

Qualified accounts are intended to be retirement accounts, and thus there are rules as to when you can, cannot, and must take money out.

For example, if you take money out of a qualified account before age fifty-nine and a half, then you must pay a penalty tax to the IRS on the withdrawal (there are some exceptions, such as withdrawing money for medical expenses).

However, even if you are not yet fifty-nine and a half, most of the time you can transfer or rollover your retirement money into a new account without paying taxes on the transfer/rollover.

Contrary to popular belief, many people can roll over or transfer retirement accounts from their present employer into other investments even while they are still working with the company that provided the account.

The reason is that the financial crisis in 2008 decimated many retirees' investment accounts, forcing them back to work. As a result, many companies began to allow their employees to move their money into accounts that they are more comfortable with. Nowadays, I help clients transfer money from accounts provided by their present employers into new investments all the time.

When it comes to withdrawing money, most qualified accounts (except for Roth IRAs) also have a "seventy-three rule," which means that you must start taking money out when you reach age seventy-three. The reason behind the rule is that the government wants you to start paying taxes on your investments—they let you defer the taxes until age seventy-three, but then they want to start collecting.

The amount that you must withdraw is called a required minimum distribution (RMD). The **tax penalty for not taking your RMD is a whopping 50 percent** of the RMD amount. Ouch!

We remind our clients each year to take their RMD to help them avoid these penalties.

Maximum contributions and maximum income restrictions

Based on your age and income, the IRS limits the amount of qualified money that you can invest each year.

A high annual income can also limit your ability to make qualified investments. Once you reach a certain level of income, your contributions become only partially tax deductible; if you hit an even higher income threshold, they are no longer tax deductible at all. The IRS adjusts these income thresholds from year to year.

Any money that you contribute to an IRA, 401(k), etc. above the maximum annual contribution limit is considered nonqualified, so you do not get to deduct it from your current tax return. However, you will not get taxed twice—when you withdraw the investment, you will only be taxed on the earnings (and not the principal) of the nonqualified portion.

Upside

- Because you are investing pretax money, you have more money available to invest, which means that your money may grow faster, compounding from a larger base.
- You can use your investment to reduce your gross taxable income to save money on taxes for the year in which you earn it.

Downside

- You must pay taxes on the entire amount of your investment when you take it out. Qualified money was never intended for big lump-sum withdrawals.

You may be better off taking money out as income over time to spread the tax liability out over time.

- There are limits on how much you can invest each year. You may check the IRS website (IRS.org) to find out the amount you may contribute to a qualified retirement account for the year in which you would like to contribute.

- There's limited flexibility for when you can and cannot withdraw money, such as early withdrawal penalties before age fifty-nine and a half and required minimum distributions at age seventy-three.

Nonqualified money

Nonqualified money means that you've paid income taxes on the money before you invested it. Therefore, you do not claim your investment as a deduction on your current tax return.

With most nonqualified accounts, you are taxed each year on the interest that you earn, even if you don't withdraw your money.

For example, say you invested $100,000 into a nonqualified five-year CD that earns 2 percent a year. You would earn $2,000 in interest in that first year and not be able to withdraw it yet.

In that case, you would pay taxes on that $2,000 in the first year of the deferral period, even though you cannot yet take the money out. Those earnings would increase your taxable income, which can impact your tax bracket.

That's how most nonqualified accounts work. Tax-deferred annuities are an exception. With tax-deferred annuities, you pay taxes only on the growth at the time you withdraw your money, and not as you earn it. As with all nonqualified accounts, you don't pay any taxes on the principal of a tax-deferred annuity when you take your money out, because it was already taxed before you invested.

Here's how it works in a practical sense: Let's say you invested $100,000 of nonqualified money into a tax-deferred fixed-indexed annuity, and at the end of ten years, the total value is $150,000. When you take the money out, you will be taxed on the $50,000 of growth as if it were regular income.

For comparison, if you withdrew the same investment from a qualified account, you would be taxed on the overall $150,000 at the time of withdrawal as if it were regular income.

Upside

- There are no required minimum distributions.
- There are no penalties for early withdrawal.
- Some accounts allow your money to grow tax-deferred, which can help it compound faster.
- You don't pay taxes on the principal of your investment at the time of withdrawal.

Downside

- You pay income tax at the time you earn money, so you may have less to invest up front.
- You cannot deduct the value of your investment from your income tax return at the time you invest.
- For non-tax-deferred accounts, you may have to pay taxes on money that you are not yet able to access.

Roth IRA: A separate category

A Roth IRA is *technically* considered qualified money, but in many ways, it works like nonqualified money. For instance, with a Roth IRA you are taxed at the time that you invest (so no deduction from your income tax return).

The key with a Roth IRA is that your **growth happens tax-free**. This means that you don't pay *any* additional taxes when you take a qualified withdrawal.

A withdrawal is considered qualified if:

1. You've had the Roth IRA for at least five years **and** any one of the following occurs:
   - You reach age fifty-nine and a half.
   - You die or become disabled.
   - You make a qualified first-time home purchase.[17]

---

17   RothIRA.com, "5 Roth IRA Withdrawal Rules You Need to Know," http://www.rothira.com/roth-ira-withdrawal-rules.

With a Roth IRA, you can remove your principal at any time without paying any additional taxes or penalties, even before age fifty-nine and a half. However, if you withdraw earnings in a nonqualified withdrawal (one that doesn't meet the standards listed above), you may have to pay penalties and taxes.[18]

One of the key benefits of a Roth IRA is that you can experience tax-free growth if you always take qualified distributions.

Let's say you made $1,000 a week. If you invested $100 of that into your Roth IRA, you would be taxed on the full $1,000 during the tax year in which you earned it. However, assuming you always take qualified distributions, those are the only taxes that you and your beneficiaries should ever pay on that investment. No matter how much your account goes up, 100 percent of your qualified withdrawals, including interest, will be tax-free.

Many investors are attracted to Roth IRAs because of their tax-free growth. It's *almost* an exclusion to the old saying that "the only two things that are certain are death and taxes." In a Roth IRA, you only pay taxes before you invest. Once the money is in, you don't pay any more taxes on it if you always take qualified distributions.

---

18 "Roth IRA Withdrawal Rules," Charles Schwab, accessed February 24, 2017, http://www.schwab.com/public/schwab/investing/ retirement_and_planning/understanding_iras/roth_ira/withdrawal_ rules.

While you don't benefit from a write-off at the time you invest, you may net more money by taking tax-free income later in life, especially if you are in a higher tax bracket when you withdraw your money.

I believe that one should not risk tax-free money. I'm always surprised when someone has a Roth IRA and it's full of stocks, bond funds, and mutual funds—why risk tax-free investments? On the other hand, investing in a fixed-indexed annuity in a Roth IRA can compound the security and growth of your money.

Upside

- It offers tax-free growth.
- You can remove your principal (but not earnings) at any time without any penalty.
- Penalty-free early withdrawal of earnings is allowed for such things as buying a first house or certain medical expenses.
- You can have tax-free qualified withdrawals.
- There are no required minimum distributions.

Downside

- There are limits on how much you can invest each year.
- There are penalties for early withdrawals of your earnings before age fifty-nine and a half.

Qualified and nonqualified, and the three types of money

Qualified money and nonqualified money are not alternatives to the three types of money; they are just labels for the tax status of your money. **You can use qualified or nonqualified accounts for all three types of money.**

Many people are confused about the difference between the tax status of their money and the type of investment that they have. This is no surprise given the misinformation surrounding the financial industry.

Many times, I'll ask someone what types of investments they have, by which I mean stocks, bonds, mutual funds, annuities, etc.

They'll say, "I have an IRA." Or, "I have a Roth IRA."

They're referring to the *tax status* of the account, which is different than what they are invested in.

You can have a *bank CD* in a Roth IRA.

You can have a *stock account* in a Roth IRA.

You can have a *fixed-indexed annuity* in a Roth IRA.

What you invest in (such as stocks, bonds funds, and fixed-indexed annuities) and how the IRS treats your money (IRA or Roth IRA) **are separate.**

Why qualified vs. nonqualified matters

The tax status of your money matters because your tax bracket will have a major impact on the percentage of your investment that you keep.

For years we've been told to put money into retirement accounts because we'll be in lower tax brackets when we retire. However, you must be careful about this, because a lot of people are in higher tax brackets when they retire, for a few reasons:

1. Taxes seem to go up all the time.
2. They're receiving Social Security and investment income, combined with fewer work-related deductions.

Considering taxes is vital to a successful investment strategy. Based on your current tax bracket and the tax brackets that you anticipate you will be in going forward, you may adjust the way that you invest to try to keep more money overall.

For example, people who will potentially be in a higher bracket when they retire may decide to invest in a Roth IRA instead of a regular qualified account.

On the other hand, working people in high income brackets often want to use contributions to their retirement accounts to lower their taxable income; choosing qualified investments can help them save on taxes.

Either way, it is important to remember that you will likely pay taxes on every investment. The only difference is *when* you pay your taxes, which can impact how much tax you pay.

Tax strategy has a lot to do with comparing your current tax bracket with the bracket you expect to be in when you retire. This is often a guessing game; you're considering the future when you're young and thinking, "How is this going to best benefit me when I retire?" The truth is, many times you don't know.

As you get closer to retirement, the picture can become a little clearer. At that point, you can often make more educated guesses. Sometimes it may make sense to move money from qualified to nonqualified accounts, and vice versa, to take advantage of potential tax savings.

Often, it's not simply a case of qualified vs. nonqualified, but *when to use both to your advantage*. Contrary to popular belief, you don't have to move all your money from one investment to another all at once; a good plan for some of your money may not be a good plan for all of it. Utilizing both qualified and nonqualified plans can help you maximize your investments and minimize your tax liability.

This is a major reason whom you work with is so important. I have seen financial professionals make decisions without realizing that they were increasing their clients' tax liability.

Meanwhile, I have worked with clients to find investments that suit their needs while lowering their tax liability. Having an advisor who can guide you on both investing *and* tax strategy can make a world of difference in the success of your investments.

Chapter 8

ANNUITY INCOME RIDERS

How did income riders come to be?

For decades, financial advisors advocated the rule of four for taking income from investments. The theory was that you could earn enough interest each year on your investments to live off for the rest of your life without losing your principal.

Then, like a thief in the night, the market corrected down **hard**. In a flash, the stock market took away that income *and* much of the principal from many retirement accounts.

People weren't happy. The American dream is not to build your nest egg over decades of hard work and disciplined saving, only to suffer as the market takes it all away, forcing you to wait ten years or longer just to get back to where you were. Only you never really do get back to where you were—those golden years you were supposed to enjoy are never coming back.

Yes—I am talking about **TIME**!

In 2000, and again in 2008, lots of people who were about to retire couldn't afford to anymore, and many retired people had to go back to work.

For many people, these market losses weren't just numbers on a ticker; the market declines wiped out their life savings, their retirement, their dreams, or their legacy.

Lots of people understandably lost faith in the market after experiencing heavy losses in 2000, waiting years to recover, and then seeing the market take a dive again in 2008. Before investing their money again, pre-retirees and retirees wanted to know that they could keep their money safe and not run out of cash during their lifetimes.

To win back skeptical clients, financial institutions created A new product, in which many Financial Professionals added a glitzy sales pitch to match: "You can have your cake and eat it too," they told us. "We've created a way that you can invest in the market and never have to worry about outliving your money."

The new product is commonly known as an "income rider" or a "living benefit." The official name, which appears on your statements, is a *guaranteed minimum income benefit (GMIB) rider*.

How's that for financial industry jargon?

What is an income rider?

An income rider is a benefit that you can add to a variable annuity or fixed annuity usually for a fee. It guarantees the investor an **income** stream for life.

Sounds good! What could be wrong with that?

The way that income riders *really* work is almost never fully disclosed or understood. There are many moving parts to income riders that are often left out in sales pitches. We'll go into detail about each limitation later in the chapter, but here's an overview:

- Income riders don't earn guaranteed interest, they **"roll up."**
- It may take **decades** before you receive any of the company's money.
- Many income riders stop growing (rolling up) as soon as you take out your first dollar.
- Many income plans **do not** increase with inflation.
- It's a living benefit only—no lump sum for beneficiaries.

- Your actual cash value (that your beneficiaries receive) can experience losses.
- Income riders carry higher fees than expected (most people who buy variable annuities tell me that their total fees are between 1 percent and 1.5 percent, but they are usually paying **more than 3 percent in fees**).
- All fees come out of the cash value—your real money. Many times, the income rider fee is calculated by using the GMIB, So if your cash value is $100,000 and the income value is $125,000, the fee for the income rider is NOT based on your actual cash value, the $100,000. It is based on your $125,000 GMIB.

Despite these limitations, financial professionals often recommend variable annuities with income riders even to clients who don't need them, falsely claiming that the clients' investments are safe from market losses and they will earn a guaranteed interest rate. It's quite effective: If both of those things were true, why would anyone say no to an income rider?

Unfortunately, those claims are not true (as we will cover later in the chapter). The only guaranteed benefit in an income rider is a fixed stream of annual lifetime income payments. This means that unless someone needs income, he or she probably shouldn't pay for an income rider.

Still, certain financial professionals will offer nearly everyone an income rider. Why? As they say, follow the money.

A client came into my office recently. His income was incredible and was going to remain that way. He would never need income from his investments during his lifetime. But he was **paying a fee** in his variable annuity for an income rider.

"Why are you paying for this?" I asked him.

"Why *wouldn't* I have it?" the client responded. "I'm getting a guaranteed interest rate!"

Therein lies the problem. Income riders are often marketed as providing guaranteed interest rates—but they don't.

In fact, the Iowa Department of Insurance, for instance, sent a memo to all Iowa insurance companies, calling the marketing of these income riders "misleading."[19]

Specifically, the memo mentions that marketers are "emphasizing high-interest lifetime withdrawal benefit riders. Some of the advertising claim the withdrawal benefit rider has an annual rate of return, e.g., 'client earns 8%.' This statement is misleading if the consumer is not equally informed of the restrictions imposed by the rider."

The **Iowa Department of Insurance labeled "client earns" claims** that are used to market income riders as **misleading** because they are.

Income riders only make it *look* as if you earn a guaranteed interest rate on your policy, such as 5 percent, 6 percent, or even 7 percent. The reality is very different (as we'll cover soon).

---

19   Terry E. Branstad, Kim Reynolds, Nick Gerhart, "Bulletin 14-02," State of Iowa, September 15, 2014.

Many people with income riders believe that when the term expires they can take the income benefit money as a lump sum, or that if they pass away, their beneficiaries will receive the lump sum of the income benefit.

That is not the case.

However, it's hard to separate fact from fiction when it comes to income riders. The first time I heard about income riders, I was sitting in a room full of **financial advisors, and *none of them* caught on to the catches**. Wait till you hear this.

When I first heard about income riders: Finding the facts

I was invited to a luncheon by a company that wanted to share with me and other financial advisors a new fantastic way to give clients a guaranteed interest rate in a safe investment that provided lifetime income.

Wow, I thought. This was a very popular insurance company giving a presentation on a new, almost magical rider that you could—for a price—add to your annuity product.

A couple of men from the provider company stood at the front of the room and gave their pitch: "What if you could guarantee your clients 10 percent a year?" (Today, because interest rates have gone down, they'll say something more like 5 percent or 7 percent).

Of course, this got my attention. I envisioned potential clients lined up outside my door—and all the good I could do for them, including myself and my parents.

The presenters went on to tell us that the company would guarantee a 10 percent return to every client who bought its variable annuity. They then went on to illustrate how this would work.

"If a client buys one of our variable annuities for $100,000, they will earn 10 percent simple interest on their deposit, which would be $10,000 a year. Therefore, in ten years the client is guaranteed to have $200,000 in their account."

Amazing, I thought. *In ten years, you can double your money!*

They weren't done pitching either. "Beyond that, the client could also get $10,000 a year for life."

Are you kidding?! I wondered. I scanned the room full of advisors. Everyone was giddy. We were just handed a way to guarantee our clients 10 percent annually *and* give them income that they could never outlive. It felt like perfection was finally here, and we were the lucky few to be able to provide it first.

Still, the skeptic inside me wasn't convinced. I am a little weird in the sense that I like math. I started jotting down some numbers, and I could not wrap my head around how a company could do that.

I applied the age-old wisdom *follow the money*—and it just didn't add up. The company had to turn a profit offering this product after all their expenses, and I didn't see how that was possible.

What could they possibly be investing in that they would yield *more than 10 percent* each year so that they could pay the clients, cover their expenses, pay the advisors, **and** leave a profit for themselves?

In today's interest environment, how could a company even offer a guaranteed 5 percent, 6 percent, or 7 percent?

I was starting to sense that something was off.

My hope and skepticism warred within me. I very much wanted this to be true, *but I had to know the catch*. I raised my hand like a schoolchild, and one of the presenters called on me.

I asked, "Where does the $10,000 a year come from? Is this interest each year so that the principal remains whole?"

The gentlemen conducting the presentation were shaken, shooting furtive glances at each other in a wordless argument as to who should handle my question.

Finally, one of the men mustered the courage to proclaim, "Does it matter where it comes from? Your clients can now get $10,000 a year for life."

The other advisors in the room seemed to agree with the presenter—they were ready to get on their way and start offering this product to the public.

I still had a couple more questions.

"Does the beneficiary receive the full $200,000 when the client passes away?"

The gentlemen stared at each other in amazement that this question was asked. They could have set world records for jaw-dropping.

They were expecting me, like the rest of the financial advisors in the room, to simply be caught up in the excitement of what they were selling and not ask too many questions. Why would I question anything? This sales pitch could mean big bucks!

Frazzled, they started talking over each other, each more defensive than the last. I'll piece together the jigsaw puzzle of their response for you:

"This is not a death benefit. If you want that, sell your clients life insurance. This is a living benefit."

The first fact had appeared.

I wondered if there were more, but I took a break from asking questions for the moment—after all, we'd come here for a lunch, and I sensed that my less curious peers were getting hungry.

Everyone broke for food, and a few minutes later, one of the presenters tapped me on the shoulder and asked if he could talk to me outside.

I thought, *Great, these people recognize a smart individual who is engaging with their presentation and wants to learn more about it,* so they want to talk to me.

He walked me out to the front of the restaurant. When we got outside, the gentleman told me that I wasn't right for the product and that I could not go back inside.

Now I knew for sure that something was up. I left him with a warning: "You are leaving out the catches in what you're selling, but I will figure them out, and I will teach everyone that I meet how this product really works."

I got back to my office, obsessed with trying to discover what the presenters wanted to hide from me.

I searched the internet for information on income riders and quickly found that the information online couldn't be relied on—most of it was more misleading marketing.

So, I rolled up my sleeves for some old-school research. I reached out to some mentors in the business and directly called the companies offering income riders.

After a fair number of questions and further research, I finally pieced together the truth about income riders.

I found the facts. And boy, were they interesting.

I will share with you what I've learned so that you can better determine what you and your beneficiaries *are and are not getting* if you decide to pay a fee to add an income rider to a variable annuity.

Before I do, I want to say don't feel bad if you've been taken in by the marketing surrounding these products! It's often misleading, and it's so effective that even *many financial professionals don't see behind the smoke and mirrors.* My opinion in what I see is the companies describe the income rider in full detail, but it still can be confusing. Brokers and agents, or even a customer's understanding, may not be correct. But many times I hear of the income rider's rollup being offered as a guaranteed interest rate, which is not correct.

How income riders really work

An annuity with an income rider is split into two separate dollar values:

- Cash value (this is sometimes referred to as AV, or accumulation value)
- Guaranteed minimum income benefit value (GMIB) rider

The **cash value is your real money.** The income benefit value is what the company *can* use to calculate your monthly income. **I like to call the income benefit "Monopoly money."** Your beneficiaries do not receive the income benefit as a lump sum if something happens to you and you pass away. Unless, for an additional fee, you add a death benefit rider to your policy, your beneficiaries will most likely receive the cash value when you pass away, even if it is lower than your income benefit value. All these fees add up. Its practitioners will tell you the fees don't matter because you are getting a guaranteed rate of return of 5 percent, 6 percent, or 7 percent. They take the fees from your cash value. Remember the cash value is what your spouse or other beneficiary will receive when you pass away.

Say you invest $100,000 in a variable annuity and you purchase an income rider. The $100,000 doesn't grow at a 10 percent interest rate. What it does is called a "rollup." A 10 percent rollup on a $100,000 investment means that the income benefit value will rise by $10,000 a year during the deferral period (before you start withdrawing money). $100,000 rolling up by 10 percent each year gives you a $200,000 income benefit value after ten years. **Your *cash* value does not increase by the rollup amount.**

Once the deferral period ends and you start withdrawing money, the income benefit most likely stops growing. Most income riders will stop rolling up once you withdraw even a single dollar or more than a certain percent, like 4 percent to 6 percent.

The income benefit value is one factor the insurance company will use to determine what your monthly income will be while you live. The other factor is called a **"payout percentage."** This is the percentage of the income benefit value that the insurance company will pay you each year, based on your age and life expectancy.

For example, if you are sixty-five years old, then they may give you 5 percent of the income benefit value each year, but if you are seventy-three, they may pay you 6 percent annually.

A typical payout is in the 5 percent range. So, if you've deferred your $100,000 for ten years to achieve a $200,000 income benefit, the company will then begin to give you $10,000 a year in income.

However, the income starts coming out of the cash value—the money that you initially put in. *The fees are also taken out of the cash value,* and if the *market has a correction, the cash value drops even further.* **Your real money is the first thing to get drained,** limiting the actual amount that you get as a return. The same is true for your beneficiaries.

If you have an emergency during the deferral period and you need to take all your money out, you can take only the cash value (not the income benefit), and you may pay a surrender charge, which is in addition to the fees they've been charging you on the account.

On top of that, unless the advisor attached yet another "death benefit" rider onto your policy (for an additional fee, of course), then when you pass on, your beneficiaries will only be able to withdraw the *cash value* in a lump sum—**not** the income benefit value.

Here's a chart of how your investment is broken down in a variable annuity with an income rider. Your statement will have two columns, like the chart below.

On the left side, you have the cash value (your real money), and on the right, you have the income benefit value (what I like to call "Monopoly money" that can become income after the deferral period).

Investment: $100,000	
Cash value (real money)	**Income benefit value (Monopoly money)**
Can go up and down based on the market's impact on the funds that you have in your variable annuity. This side operates like a market account.	Rolls up by the rollup guarantee amount (4 to 7 percent). To keep it simple, let's use an example of a 10 percent rollup to give us $200,000 after ten years.
Average fee amounts taken out of the cash value: M&E (Mortality & Expense): 1 percent to 1.5 percent Admin fee: 0.20 percent to 0.25 percent GMIB: 0.75 percent to 1 percent* Fund fees: 1 percent **Total average fees: 3.65 percent**	We gave the variable annuity company $100,000 and deferred it for **ten years.** After ten years, they start to provide us $10,000 a year in income. **Ten years later,** we have received back our initial investment of $100,000. The company has had our money for twenty years and so far, all we've received is money we had in the first place.

* Although the cash value might be lower, the fee for the income rider is typically based on the income benefit value.

Remember, managing your money is simpler than your financial professional makes it seem. Trust your gut—if something feels off, it probably is.

The average fees for a variable annuity with an income rider equal **more than 3.5 percent a year**.[20]

Remember how damaging a 1 percent fee can be to your portfolio? These funds multiply that destructive fee by *three and a half*.

Income doesn't rise with inflation

My biggest concern with income riders is that the income doesn't rise with inflation. Once you start taking money out, in most cases, the income benefit value stops rolling up, and the income payments don't rise with inflation.

The amount that you get each year doesn't go up over time with most plans. Once you start taking income, you're locked into that annual income payment for the rest of your life.

However, because of inflation, the value of your money decreases over time—$1,000 is worth more today than it will be worth ten years from now. So, if you need $1,000 to pay your bills now, you will need more than $1,000 to pay your bills in ten years, and the income rider won't provide it to you.

---

20 Tara Siegel Bernard, "Variable Annuity Plus Guaranteed Income Merits Careful Scrutiny," *New York Times*, June 19, 2015, https://www.nytimes.com/2015/06/20/your-money/variable-annuities-with-guaranteed-income-riders-require-careful-scrutiny.html.

If you make any investments with income options, you need to have an opportunity for the income to grow. Sometimes financial professionals selling variable annuities will say that it *can* grow. The problem is, there's a big difference between what *can* happen and what likely *will* happen.

An income rider's annual payouts are very unlikely ever to grow. For your income payments to grow, the market would have to go up so high that your earnings from the fund would outpace the rollup percentage *and* the fund's average 3.5 percent in fees. I have never seen it happen, and I'm not willing to rely on it happening in the future.

Living benefit only

The income rider is a living benefit and **NOT** a death benefit. In other words, the income rider can only be used for income while you're **alive.**

Chapter 9

SHOULD WE CONTINUE
THE CONVERSATION?

S ince you've read this far, you've gained some knowledge about investing as well as getting to know me.
You've discovered the truth behind many of the myths
in the market, such as the real danger of a 1 percent fee.

You've learned how to determine whom you should work
with for your personal situation and the responsibility that
each type of financial professional owes you as well as what
they may offer you.

You know the things that you can do with your money,
the importance of tax strategy, and the facts about income
riders.

Kudos to you: That's quite a strong base of knowledge!

So, what's next?

Well, that depends. If you're young and just starting to invest, it's great that you have this information early; you can take these lessons and apply them to deciding with whom to work and where to invest your money.

If you are nearing retirement or currently retired and looking to keep some money secure, then perhaps you should get in touch with me, and we can continue the conversation about how to manage your money.

I believe in educating instead of selling, so I make it a point not to pressure people into anything. Everyone should feel comfortable with the person managing their money, and I am honored when someone decides to work with me. However, if people choose not to, I will respect that and wish them the best!

Whom I help

I focus on helping people keep some or all their money secure. Generally, I work with people preparing for retirement or who have already retired. Many times, people start to consider protecting their investments as they get closer to retiring or if they have retirement accounts from a prior employer that they'd like to transfer into something safer.

Most people come to me to roll over existing accounts or invest lump sums, rather than to create accounts for monthly contributions. Some advisors work with younger people who might put away $100 a month. I don't specialize in those situations.

I can help you:

- With what I call an "old retirement account," meaning an account provided by a past employer. I can help you move that money into something safer that will make you feel more comfortable.
- Roll lump sums from retirement accounts, investment accounts, etc. into more appropriate accounts for you.
- If you have too much money sitting in the Five-Minute money accounts, you want to keep your money secure, *and* you want to earn enough to keep pace with inflation.
- If you want to protect your principal from market declines.
- If you want a long-term, reasonable rate of return on your money.
- Understand more about keeping money secure and the challenges of various investment options.
- With your estate planning.
- If you would like to discuss your current financial situation and get an honest assessment of your situation—no hard sell involved.
- If you want a second professional opinion on your investments at no charge.

Inspiring you to reach a brighter, more secure future

I want to inspire people who might feel jaded about the system or who have been misled by anyone in the past. I make it a point to tell people the things that many won't tell them, or don't want them to know, and to teach them what is behind the smoke and mirrors.

I understand that no one makes the right decision all the time, and you may have made some financial decisions that you wish you could take back.

Don't worry: Whatever has happened before, we're here to help you try to fix it.

While it's natural to feel embarrassed if your investments haven't performed the way you'd hoped—especially if you find out that you may have made a mistake—I want you to know that when you come in to our office, **I will never make you feel embarrassed.**

I know how hard the industry makes investing. I understand that you can be smart, hard-working, honest, caring, and an expert of your craft, and *still* make a bad investment or fall prey to an alluring sales pitch.

Don't beat yourself up about it. It's OK.

The industry is built on information, and it is very easy to fall into the trap and make a decision that can harm your financial future.

Still, *it's never too late.*

I believe I have the financial knowledge to help you out of a tight spot. Even if you feel that you haven't made the right financial decisions so far, we can help you make better ones going forward.

Come in to see me, and you'll find a financial professional who respects you, who will take the time to help you understand everything that your money is doing—including the things that your last financial professional may have glossed over. **If you are worried about something, even if you don't quite know how to talk about it, please give us a call.**

While it is understandable to feel embarrassed, if you don't speak up, then any negative trends you're experiencing can continue to get worse.

Trust your gut. If something feels off, it probably is—even if you don't know why. Let us know what you feel, and we can help you understand and do our best to solve the problem or problems.

My unique skill is the ability to help you understand your investments, including the misconceptions, and to find the right solutions for *you*—not for me.

As I stated earlier, I am never the smartest guy in the room. I do, however, know how to help you with your objectives and goals. I cannot walk into your profession and do what you do—it would most likely take years of training, research, and commitment. That is exactly what I have given my career, and I'm here to help you. If you want me to I will and if you don't, I won't.

How I serve my clients

We put our clients first at my company.

In our office, integrity means that if we say something, we believe it, and we demonstrate it with our actions. While no individual or company is perfect, we strive to make our communications and actions consistent and to deliver on what we promise.

We create a welcoming atmosphere for all our clients, so that they know we're on their team to support them. We've had clients come here and use our fax machine. Others have come to our office to access the internet on their laptop. My assistants are licensed notaries, so we can do notaries for clients, too. We're all about **people helping people.**

When you need support, we're there for you.

I hear all the time that financial professionals won't call their clients back for days at a time, which is crazy to me in today's age of technology.

When our clients call us, we call them back right away.

With modern technology, it's easy to return a phone call or message. So, I call clients back as soon as I can, even on weekends. Many clients aren't used to such a quick response time from their financial professionals.

I am happy to call clients back right away, not because it's my job but because **I can soothe their worries and make**

their lives more peaceful—just by giving them a quick phone call.

How lucky am I?

Many people work with financial professionals based on a personal relationship. They had a friend or family member in the business, so they turned to them to manage their money or even a percentage of it. While it's nice to help a friend out, it can also create some tension—after all, your life savings is serious business!

I respect my clients and want them to see me as a professional. Don't get me wrong, my clients and I are very friendly. We may have lunch or play golf, but I always respect them enough to be professional.

I want them to be able to fire me if they are not happy. I won't play the friend card in a tough situation, because I respect my clients' desire for professionalism.

Not all financial professionals are in the business for the long haul.

I created this company to be transparent, friendly, and informative; to be a **one-stop shop for your investments, insurance, and tax strategy.** We can do any one or all of those things for you.

I already have a financial professional. Why do I need Doug?

Most people who visit us are already working with financial professionals. We are not trying to steal you away from them.

Whether we will work together or not, I encourage you to educate yourself about your investments, to find out what risk level you feel good about, and to work with people whom you like and trust and who know what they're doing.

My goal is to teach you about your options, so that you can feel confident about what you are doing with your money.

I'm not trying to fit a square peg into a round hole. When I meet new clients, and go over their finances with them, I give an honest assessment of where they are and what I think they should do—even if that means I won't make a dime from them.

I have advised many people with whom I've met, to keep what they have, if it meets their goals and needs, and not move any money into accounts that I manage. I didn't make any money from those meetings, but I feel good knowing that I'm serving their best interests. That's the way it is supposed to be.

When you contact me, you're not signing up for a hard sell. I will give you an honest, thorough look at your finances and priorities and offer advice from there—even if that advice means that I don't make any money.

My integrity is worth more to me than money from a client who doesn't need to spend it. I'm always happy to look over people's investments and help them understand what's happening with their money.

Many times, people come to me when they just have a bad feeling about what's going on with their investments, but they can't quite put their finger on why.

You'd be surprised how many times their gut feelings are spot on. Many times, when people come to see me because something doesn't feel right, it's not that they don't understand what's happening—it's that *something is not right*.

If you feel uncomfortable, even if you don't know why, I am happy to look at your investments for you and give you my opinion.

If I see that your investable money is in a place that is working best for you, I will tell you just that. I won't recommend making changes just to make changes. If I see that I may be able to put you in a better position for retirement, then I will recommend a solution.

What I like to do for you

What I want you to get from this book is the confidence that you know what your money is doing, or at the very least, you understand your money better. I have the same goal when advising clients.

I will always be direct with you, and I will educate you on the benefits and the limitations of anything that I recommend or what you currently hold.

I will not compromise my morals or ethics for anybody— not for any client, and not for any company.

I like to help you:

- Roll over or transfer your existing retirement accounts into a Protection with Power plan.
- Secure your principal for the future.
- Implement a good tax strategy so you can keep as much of your investment money as possible.
- Create a complete package to help you manage your money.
- Find safer investments.
- Get out of investments that have too many costs and fees.
- Find products that provide income for retirement that will increase.
- Find solutions for making back "old money"— money that you already had before the market took it away from you.
- Manage investments in the market.
- Keep what you have.

I strive to help you recognize **real** security and benefits, not the hypothetical safety offered by financial professionals putting your money in bond funds or attaching income riders that you may not need.

I work to help you understand the risks that you are choosing to undertake or to avoid, so that you can feel comfortable with your retirement accounts.

What you can expect when you contact me

If you want to reach out to me, you can get in touch any time at doug@cswta.net. I respond to emails quickly, and I love to be there for clients both old and new.

When you do get in touch, I will do my best to answer your questions. We can even set up a no-pressure, face-to-face, second professional opinion meeting, so we can get to know each other.

A meeting with me is much more of a collaboration than a sales pitch. I'm not a salesperson. I am an educator.

I run my own outfit, so my job is not to sell you any specific product. I didn't get into this business to sell things—I started my company to empower people to reach their investment and retirement goals.

When you come meet with me, we will have a discussion to discover what you may need. That discovery is the first step in creating the right plan for you.

There is no cookie-cutter financial product that works for everyone. Some are for income. Some are for death benefits. Some are for accumulation. Some are for all three or a combination.

Once we understand what your goals are, then I will show a way to make that happen in collaboration with you. If I can help you, great. If your needs are outside of what I specialize in I will tell you that too.

If you come to see me, you should expect that we will go over your priorities and financial position, and we'll explore what you want. Before I recommend anything, it's important that I can find out a little bit about you and share a little bit about me.

Some people come in and don't know their financial position or their priorities. That's OK.

If you are unsure about your position or your priorities, then I'll ask you some questions to open your mind and help you figure out what your priorities are, or maybe even what your priorities should be, based on your situation.

I'll go over the types of money with you, and **you'll have the opportunity to ask me any questions you like.**

Together, we'll figure it out.

I feel that my job is to uncover things that you may not know are concerns for you and to come up with solutions *before* problems arise. That way you're proactive and ahead of the game, and we can address issues from a position of strength.

I celebrate the opportunity to educate and provide support, even for those who do not become clients of mine. Some advisors charge (quite a lot) hourly to evaluate someone's investments and give advice.

I provide free consultations to potential clients. If you have something that's working well for you, I'm happy to tell you as much, even if it means I don't get any business from our meeting. At the end of the day, **I want you to feel good after meeting with me and to know more about money**

when you leave my office than you did when you came in. If I can help you, I will.

When you meet with me, we'll go over your finances, and I'll do my best to educate you in any area in which you need clarity. As you close this book, and at the end of our meeting, it's important to ask yourself four questions before deciding if you want to continue the conversation:

1. Do I like this guy?
2. Can I trust this guy?
3. Does this guy know what he's doing?
4. What is my gut telling me?

At the end of the day, it's as simple as that.

ABOUT THE AUTHOR

Doug Clancy grew up in New Hampshire, where his father and mother taught him the value of working hard, of integrity, of speaking honestly and plainly, and of always doing the right thing for others. This laid the foundation for Doug's career in the financial industry, where Doug has put his clients first for more than twenty years.

Doug founded Retirement Planning Services, Inc. (doing business as Cornerstone Wealth and Tax Advisory in California). To this day, Doug runs his business with the purpose of helping clients protect their money. Along the way, he works to teach them the pros and cons of every investment they consider, so that every client can find the right solutions for his or her individual situation.

Doug is an investment advisor representative, tax advisor, and insurance agent—a rarity in this business. Doug's unique knowledge of the industry springs from his desire to be able to serve his clients by understanding and sharing knowledge about the financial industry at large—not just about what he sells.

HOW TO GET IN TOUCH WITH DOUG

Email: Doug@cswta.net
Phone: (916) 596-0500

A free ebook edition is available with the purchase of this book.

To claim your free ebook edition:

1. Visit MorganJamesBOGO.com
2. Sign your name CLEARLY in the space
3. Complete the form and submit a photo of the entire copyright page
4. You or your friend can download the ebook to your preferred device

A **FREE** ebook edition is available for you or a friend with the purchase of this print book.

_____

CLEARLY SIGN YOUR NAME ABOVE

Instructions to claim your free ebook edition:
1. Visit MorganJamesBOGO.com
2. Sign your name CLEARLY in the space above
3. Complete the form and submit a photo of this entire page
4. You or your friend can download the ebook to your preferred device

Print & Digital Together Forever.

Snap a photo   Free ebook   Read anywhere

Printed in the USA
CPSIA information can be obtained
at www.ICGtesting.com
JSHW082339140824
68134JS00020B/1770

9 781683 505693